Cheltenham Town FC

Town FC

Classic Matches

Cheltenham Town FC

Classic Matches

JON PALMER

The
History
Press

First published 2009

The History Press
The Mill, Brimscombe Port
Stroud, Gloucestershire, GL5 2QG
www.thehistorypress.co.uk

© Jon Palmer, 2009

The right of Jon Palmer to be identified as the Author
of this work has been asserted in accordance with the
Copyrights, Designs and Patents Act 1988.

British Library Cataloguing in Publication Data.
A catalogue record for this book is available from the British Library.

ISBN 978 0 7524 4711 7

Printed in Great Britain

Foreword by John Finnigan

When Jon asked me to write a foreword for this book I felt very privileged and I saw it as a great honour to accept. In the book we are taken down memory lane as we remember some of the greatest games in Cheltenham Town's illustrious history. Jon has filled the book with the sort of games which make you proud to be a Robin, whether you're a supporter, a member of staff or a player. Just reading through the match reports will I'm sure evoke fantastic memories and have Cheltenham fans feeling a great deal of pleasure looking back at some of the club's finest achievements.

I first met Jon in 2006 when he was introduced as the *Gloucestershire Echo's* football writer who would be covering the club's on- and off pitch events. I soon realised that it wasn't just a job for Jon, it was also his passion. He was researching and writing about the club he had supported all of his life. Jon has built up some strong relationships with both players and backroom staff at the club, he is highly respected and a member of the local press who the squad are always willing to give time to as someone we can trust. Nobody could argue with Jon's credentials as the right man to write this book.

The book gives a great insight into each individual match chosen, but also a lesson into the history of the club and where it came from. Matches spanning back to the 1930s and up to the present day are what have helped shape the history of this fine club and it is a reminder of how far this club has come to get where it is today.

When Steve Cotterill signed me back in 2002 I had no idea what was ahead but it proved to be the most rewarding move I could have wished for. Within three months I found myself in the club's first ever play-off campaign. Having beaten Hartlepool after two legs and a nerve-wracking penalty shoot-out we were matched up against old rivals Rushden & Diamonds; for the winners would be a place in football's third tier for the first time in history. We won the game comfortably with a 3–1 scoreline and celebrated the victory with a lap of honour to share our adulation with 16,000 or so ecstatic Cheltenham fans who had made the trip to Cardiff.

The club matched this achievement four years later as John Ward guided our young squad to play-off glory once again, beating Wycombe Wanderers over two legs before overcoming Grimsby 1–0 in the magnificent Millennium Stadium. Captaining the side that day and lifting the trophy was the best day of my footballing life and I consider myself very fortunate to have lifted that trophy on behalf of Cheltenham Town Football Club and for this the club will always be in my heart.

Other moments that fill me with pride have been the opportunities to lead the team out against Premiership opposition, namely Fulham, Sunderland and who could forget the day Alan Shearer took to the Whaddon Road turf for giants Newcastle United in the FA cup fourth round in front of the BBC TV cameras.

Huge games before my time at Whaddon Road are arguably the biggest and most important the club have ever taken part in. Cheltenham fans and ex-players have waxed lyrically during my time here about epics against both Rushden & Diamonds and Yeovil Town in the Conference, and also the winning visit to Wembley's famous twin towers against Southport in 1998. These are the sort of matches that have put Cheltenham Town FC on the map. Let's hope in the coming years the club can continue to grow further and compete in many more games of this magnitude.

MATCH 1: CARLISLE UNITED V. CHELTENHAM TOWN

FA Cup Second Round
Saturday 9 December 1933, Brunton Park
Carlisle United 1 (Slinger) Cheltenham Town 2 (Smith, Bradley og)

Cheltenham Town earned a famous victory over Football League opposition in the 1933/34 FA Cup, and they would have to wait for more than sixty years to achieve that feat again. A first round win over Barnet put the wheels in motion for Cheltenham's finest run in the FA Cup until 2001/02, when they reached the fifth round under Steve Cotterill's incredible managerial reign. They had reached round three again in 1997/98, when they lost to Reading after a replay.

The 1930s were a significant period for Cheltenham, who moved to Whaddon Road in 1932 having already become 'the Robins' after their switch from ruby shirts to red and white. The club also joined the Birmingham Combination.

Street, Merthyr and Calne & Harris United were all disposed of in the qualifying rounds by a rampant Robins side, who beat Calne 10–1 at Whaddon Road. However, they were actually beaten 2–1 by Llanelli after a replay in the third qualifying round, only to be given a reprieve as the Welsh club were thrown out of the competition for fielding an ineligible player.

Cheltenham thrashed Barnet 5–1 in the opening round proper before a record Whaddon Road crowd of about 6,000. The scorers were Horace Payne (2), George Knight (2) and Harold Yarwood.

Their reward was a long trip north west to Carlisle United's Brunton Park for a second round clash and they recorded a famous upset, defeating the Cumbrians 2–1. Neither the Third Division status of their opponents, nor the fact they were playing away at a ground much bigger than those on which they usually play, daunted Town, whose brilliant defence, aided by the forwards' ability to make the most of their chances, enabled the team to achieve the biggest triumph of their careers.

The crowd disagreed on numerous occasions with the decisions of Mr R.K. Warburton, of Bolton, Lancashire, the referee, and towards the finish of the game showed their disapproval. At the final whistle, several hundreds swarmed onto the field and threatened to mob the referee. Officials and police quickly formed an escort and Mr Warburton was safely accompanied to the dressing room.

Cheltenham took to the field without George Knight, who had a knee injury. Heavy rain fell at Carlisle in the early hours of the morning and with the pitch on the soft side, the selectors put Reg

Cheltenham Town's first team of giantkillers before the big cup tie.

Smith at inside right, he being best-suited to the conditions. Blackburn, the captain, received several wires wishing the Town luck, including one from Tamworth FC.

The game kicked off in dull conditions, with practically no wind. Blackburn lost the toss, which he had made a habit of, and Yarwood kicked off before more than 7,000 spectators. Turner shot wide in the first minute and Cheltenham were soon defending. Carlisle were pulled up for a foul on Lang, but this brought no relief. Davis made a great save from Slinger. Play was kept in midfield for some time after this and the ball came across to Slinger again, but he lifted it too high. Blackburn defended strongly. The first corner came after 12 minutes. Blackburn had to kick behind. Cheltenham weathered Carlisle's storming tactics and at last went on the attack as Smith shot wide.

Carlisle played a long passing game, but Cheltenham managed to nip their movements in the bud. United played the ball to Slinger continuously, but he was well marked by Blackburn and Williams. Carlisle had most of the play territorially, but the Town gave nothing away. McBain was winded temporarily. Davis saved a grand shot from Slinger and at the other end, Yarwood tested Wolf.

Cheltenham now began to carry the fight to the home team. The Town forced a corner on Hill's wing, but the ball was put behind. A chance was missed here. Smith was playing well in Knight's place and Carlisle were weak in front of goal. Cheltenham still had to defend hard and from short range Kennedy put in the best shot of the match which passed outside the upright. Wolf came out and saved well from Hill. Cheltenham, however, worried Carlisle's defence after this, but Legge and Bradley were stout defenders. Wolf saved a fine low cross drive sent in by Smith. Stevenson got in a great shot which was deflected by a Town player for a corner, but nothing came of the kick.

Jones was pulled up for a foul near the touch line, but Williams cleared the free-kick. Another free-kick followed for Carlisle, but after many men had placed the ball in the goalmouth, Turner put over the top. Williams played a great defensive game, helping Cheltenham out of many situations. Fifty seconds before the half-time whistle, Slinger received the ball just outside the Cheltenham goal area and with two or three Town players around him, he crashed the ball into the back of the net. Cheltenham trailed at the break and Carlisle had done most of the pressing, but to little avail.

The football was most exciting and Williams was a thorn in the Carlisle attack. United forced another corner, but Goodger cleared. There was more cohesion about Cheltenham in the second half as they seemed to become more accustomed to the big ground and the thrill of the large crowd and Reg Smith scored the equalising goal. Blake rattled the crossbar for Carlisle with a terrific shot and Davis saved magnificently from McBain.

The ball became soft and had to be changed and Kennedy was sent off after an incident. Carlisle had appeals for a penalty turned down. Hill then missed with only Wolf to beat. Yarwood then set up Hill, but Wolf ran out to save and Bradley, in his anxiety to clear, pushed the ball into his own goal. Hill had applied great pressure and was responsible for the scoring of the goal, which came only a minute from the end of the game.

Carlisle had one more chance, but they bustled Davis into the net with the ball and a free-kick was given as Cheltenham held out for the most significant result in their early history.

The bell-ringers of the parish church were ringing a merry peal when the result of Cheltenham's success came over the wires. It synchronised well with the occasion and breathed the happy spirit with which the news was received in the town. Everyone was delighted with the Town's triumph and in the streets, supporters gathered eagerly awaiting the result, perhaps not with a little anxiety after the half-time scores and there were exultant shouts of 'Bravo, Cheltenham!' The gate money from the match was £371 19s 9d.

Carlisle United: Wolf, Bradley, Legge, Blake, Kennedy, Clark, McBain, Gray, Slinger, Stevenson, Turner.
Cheltenham Town: Davis, Jones, Harris, Lang, Blackburn, Goodger, Payne, Smith, Yarwood, Evans, Hill.
Attendance: 7,437.

MATCH 2: CHELTENHAM TOWN V. BLACKPOOL

FA Cup Third Round
Saturday 13 January 1934, Cheltenham Athletic Ground
Cheltenham Town 1 (Payne 5)
Blackpool 3 (Bussey, Watson 59 pen, Doherty 77)

Having stunned Carlisle United in the second round of the FA Cup, Cheltenham Town were rewarded with a third-round tie against Blackpool and the match attracted the biggest crowd ever to watch the Robins in their home town. The town's Mayor, Cllr E. Ward, was among the small party of visitors to the offices of the *Gloucestershire Echo* to see the arrival of the news of the big draw. Cheltenham's chairman, vice chairman, treasurer and other members of the committee were also present. Cheltenham were drawn out late and when the tapes announced that they were drawn at home against Blackpool, a leading side in the Second Division of the English League, there was much satisfaction. The Mayor said before the game, 'I think it is a wonderful achievement for a young team like Cheltenham to go to the front rank. Although I am myself a follower of rugby, I am naturally interested in the progress of the town's football club and I wish them every success against Blackpool. I certainly hope the club will be able to find the necessary accommodation for the match to be played in Cheltenham. Everyone, I am sure, will hope that.'

The middle pages of Cheltenham Town's first FA Cup third-round programme.

Blackpool had been relegated from the top flight the previous season and the unprecedented interest in the match meant it was switched to the Cheltenham Athletic Ground, which could accommodate far more spectators than Whaddon Road. The people of Cheltenham and the surrounding area came out in force on the big day. No sporting event in Cheltenham's history had captured the imagination of the public as the FA Cup run of 1933/34 had. Only about 300 fans were expected to make the trip down from Blackpool, but elaborate preparations were made to cope with the influx of football enthusiasts from far and wide and even special road and rail facilities were provided. Special train services were put on by the London, Midland & Scottish Railway from, not only Blackpool, but from Birmingham, Bristol, Redditch, Evesham, Malvern and Worcester as well. The Great Western Railway ran special excursion trains covering all districts including Swindon, Hereford, Cardiff, Worcester and the Forest of Dean. All trains passed through the St James' station, which was only a short walk from the Athletic Ground. Double-decker buses picked up all arrivals at the Midland station at which, of course, all Blackpool supporters arrived, and ran straight to the ground. Special parking arrangements were made for the area around the ground and for one day only, Cheltenham became a footballing Mecca.

More than 4,000 advance tickets were sold by 12.30 p.m. on the day before the big match. All the stand accommodation had been booked and Cheltenham Football League matches were postponed to allow players to watch the Blackpool tie. More than 10,000 supporters descended on the Robins' temporary home to witness history in the making.

'The Town', as they were more often to referred to in those days, put up a great fight, but their cup adventure was finally ended by Blackpool, who ran out 3–1 winners. Payne's goal gave Cheltenham the lead within five minutes of the start, raising hopes of another upset. However, the superior class of the Seasiders told in the second half and although the defence, particularly Davis in goal, put in some fine work, the Town's resistance was overcome.

The only people in Cheltenham who were not moved to great excitement by the cup tie were the two teams who were to take part in the match. The Blackpool players remained in bed until 11 a.m. after an early morning cup of tea, while several Cheltenham players carried on with their work as normal. Referee Mr Stockbridge inspected the ground in the morning and expressed himself as highly satisfied with all the arrangements and appointments. Cheltenham were first out and got a great reception from the crowd three minutes before kick-off was due. They were followed closely by Blackpool in Oxford and Cambridge blue stripes.

Blackburn won the toss and Cheltenham defended the Albion Street end goal with the wind at their backs. It was dull and overcast when Doherty kicked off before the big crowd. Cheltenham attacked from the start and McDonough had to handle. Within a minute the town forced a corner following fine work by Payne. Then Blackpool burst away on the left, but Jones ran forward and snapped up the ball to put Cheltenham on the attack again. Roy Hill put over a fine centre and Blackpool conceded a corner. Hill took the kick and with the ball going right across the goalmouth, Payne came tearing up to meet it and headed it in to put Cheltenham ahead in the fifth minute. Blackpool improved and they forced a corner that was cleared. Blackburn plied Payne with another nice pass, the movement broke down at Knight. Davis made a great save from Doherty and a minute later the same player put the ball in the net, but was pulled up for offside.

There was a typical cup tie atmosphere and Davis performed heroics to keep Cheltenham 1–0 ahead at half-time. Cheltenham lacked fire in their play early in the second half, playing against the breeze, and after one or two defensive mistakes, Bussey drove in a fine shot to make it 1–1. Davis made yet another good save from Bussey, but Watson added Blackpool's second from the penalty spot in the fifty-ninth minute.

A goal down, Cheltenham did not give up hope, but Williams had to kick off his own goal line to prevent a third for Blackpool. The Town had another spell on the attack, but it was short-lived and Blackpool were soon exerting great pressure again. Davis saved well from Tom Jones before, at the other end, Yarwood threatened, but Blackpool did well to clear. Doherty headed against the crossbar, and then in the seventy-seventh minute, he received the ball in the middle and beat Blackburn before driving in a great shot to beat Davis in the far corner.

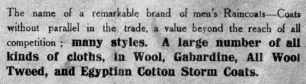
The front cover of the big match programme for the visit of Blackpool.

The result was no longer in doubt, but Cheltenham plugged away. Blackpool wasted several other good opportunities, but they kept Cheltenham defending hard. Right at the end Payne put the ball over for Yarwood to rise to hit. He bowled the 'keeper over but a defender cleared and it finished 3–1 in the Seasiders' favour.

Cheltenham had to wait until January 1998 to play another match at the third round stage of the FA Cup. The attendance of 10,389 remains the highest crowd to watch the team play in Cheltenham.

Cheltenham Town: Davis, Jones, Williams, Long, Blackburn, Goodger, Payne, Knight, Yarwood, Evans, Hill.
Blackpool: McDonough, Everest, Wassall, S. Jones, Watson, Dougall, Smailes, T. Jones, Bussey, Rattray.
Attendance: 10,389.

MATCH 3: CHELTENHAM TOWN V. READING

FA Cup First Round
Saturday 17 November 1956, Whaddon Road
Cheltenham Town 1 (McAllister 15) Reading 2 (Dixon 44, 77)

Whaddon Road's record crowd saw Cheltenham Town go down fighting against Reading in an FA Cup first round tie in 1956. The Robins had knocked out Lovells Athletic, Ebbw Vale, Gloucester City, Llanelli and Andover in the qualifying rounds.

Jim McAllister scored for Cheltenham in the fifteenth minute and Dixon netted both goals for Reading. McAllister joined Cheltenham after two seasons at Millwall. He had previously played for Glasgow junior club Neilson Victoria. The previous season had seen Cheltenham finish second in the Southern League – the highest position they had achieved, but not since they played Blackpool twenty-two years earlier had there been such interest in a Robins game. The Robins brought back Augie Scott in place of Mitchinson at inside right. Jim Geddes, who broke a couple of bones in his right-hand in the match against the RAF Home Command, had his plaster removed the day before the game, but he was not fit to play. There was a doubt over twenty-year-old left winger Clive Burder,

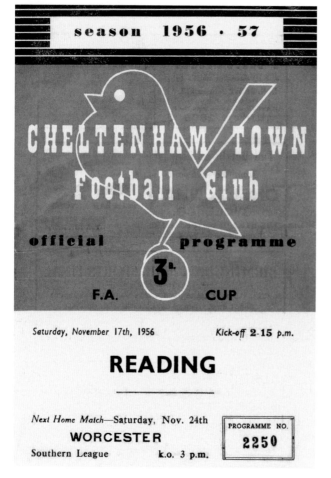

season 1956 · 57

CHELTENHAM TOWN
Football Club

official   programme

3ᵈ·

F.A.   CUP

Saturday, November 17th, 1956   Kick-off 2-15 p.m.

READING

Next Home Match—Saturday, Nov. 24th
WORCESTER
Southern League   k.o. 3 p.m.

PROGRAMME NO.
2250

The front cover of the programme for Whaddon Road's highest crowd.

CHELTENHAM TOWN (Red and White Shirts)

RIGHT]   [LEFT
1 GOURLAY

2 McDONALD   3 BAIRD

4 FARREL   5 HYDE   6 DUNN

7 CLELAND   8 SCOTT   9 McALLISTER   10 KEEN   11 BURDER

Referee :   Linesmen :
Mr. L. Callaghan (Merthyr Tydfil)   Mr. A. Owen (Coventry)
                                           Mr. J. H. Hobson (Kidderminster)

11 WHEELER   10 CRONIN   9 DIXON   8 WHITEHOUSE   7 CAMPBELL

6 EVANS   5 SPIERS   4 ANDERTON

3 REEVES   2 McLAREN

LEFT]   RIGHT]
1 MEESON

READING

How the teams lined up for the first-round tie.

who was posted to an army training course in Aldershot, but manager Arch Anderson went to Aldershot to obtain permission for the Welsh Schoolboy international to play and for him to travel back to Cheltenham the evening before the match.

The Robins had an extra training session in preparation for the game, training three evenings instead of two. Bulldozers were at Whaddon Road all week heaping up ashes on top of the banking to make room for more spectators. A crash barrier was erected at the bottom end of the ground as a safety precaution and several hundred railway sleepers were piled up to make additional terracing at the corners of the ground. The Whaddon recreation ground was made available for parking. As early as 11.30 a.m. spectators began to stream into the ground for the big game, which kicked off at 2.15 p.m. The early arrivals were all holders of ground tickets and they arrived in good time in order to obtain the best possible position from which to watch the match. Right up to kick-off the remaining tickets were being sold at the turnstiles.

Mr H.W. Compton, chairman of the Robins' board of directors, received several letters and telegrams wishing the Cheltenham team luck. One was a telegram from Old Patesians RFC. It read, 'Best of luck Robins in your game. Different ball, same town.' Lovells Athletic also sent a letter of best wishes. An amusing sideline was the number of banners in red and white colours proclaiming 'Up the Robins' which appeared from nowhere and were fastened to the stands' supports.

The Reading team arrived soon after 1 p.m. and it was learned that they were to make one change. Bobbie Campbell, their former Scottish international outside-right had injured his groin against Millwall the previous Saturday and was unable to turn out. Penford, a regular member of the Reading side, took his place. Harry Johnson, the Reading manager, said he was looking forward to a good game.

'It will not be easy,' he said. 'These games never are.' Reading travelled overnight and stayed at the Crown Hotel, Cirencester. The Robins selected Scott at inside-right and John Farrel at right-half.

The crowd continued to pour into the ground, among them 500 Reading supporters, and by half an hour before kick-off there were already about 6,000 fans present. Crowd stewards with megaphones were needed to pack the spectators. The Cheltenham Silver Band played selections as the crowd assembled. There was a great roar from a crowd numbering well over 8,000 when Farrel led the Robins out. There was also a good cheer for Reading, led by a mascot and wearing blue and white colours. Farrel tossed the coin and Reeves, winning the toss, chose to defend the Whaddon Road end.

In the first minute, McAllister was fouled inches outside the Reading penalty area, but Spiers headed the resulting free-kick clear. Then the Robins won a corner, Reeves deflecting Cleland's centre over the goal line. Things looked threatening for Reading when Scott put over another dangerous corner but McAllister was pulled up for an infringement. The Robins were on top and soon collected another corner, Reeves again giving it away. Following the corner, Farrel tried a piledriver shot which was well wide of the mark. McAllister was again fouled, Burder took the kick and Meeson rose up to save splendidly; McAllister however, was offside. Reading nearly scored in the tenth minute, Gourlay making a heroic save from Dixon, who was allowed to burst clean through the middle. A third corner came the Robins' way in the fifteenth minute and from it they took the lead to shock the Third Division club. Scott took the kick and placed the ball beautifully on Cleland's head. The Robins right-winger headed the ball goalwards and McAllister met the ball cleanly with his head to send the ball into the Reading net, past the helpless Meeson.

The Robins maintained the initiative, and a few minutes later, Meeson was forced to make a great save to keep out a Cleland header. Cleland, signed from Scottish Junior club Newarthill Hearts in October 1954, was, as usual, playing a brilliant game on the right wing and had the measure of Reeves, the Reading skipper. In the defence, Joe Hyde, at centre-half, was as determined as ever and Reading found it difficult to get past him. Only a goal-line clearance by McLaren, the Reading left-back, prevented the Robins from scoring again. Scott put over a low centre, Meeson was hustled by Cleland and McLaren cleared only just in time with the ball about to cross the line.

Reading had a few opportunities and when Dixon tried a shot, Gourlay made a remarkable point-blank save. Reading regained their stride and when the forwards took part in a pretty movement, the whole Robins defence was drawn out. Wheeler, the Reading left winger, was left unmarked, but Hyde came across to make a wonderful sliding tackle to relieve the pressure. The Robins then launched another attack on the Reading goal, just failing to send the ball home after several goalmouth scrambles.

Reading were coming to life and they won a fruitless corner, but the Robins were defending well with inside-forwards Scott and Keen helping out. McDonald made two excellent tackles to rob Wheeler of the ball and Gourlay saved well from Cronin. Reading forced a corner and it was from this that they equalised after the Robins had held them out under pressure. A minute before the interval, Wheeler, the Reading left-winger, took the kick on the left and centre-forward Dixon headed home. It was odd that both goals had come in exactly the same way. The score was 1–1 at half-time, although the Robins had had the edge over their opponents during the first half.

Reading played some good football on the resumption. Dixon drew the Robins' defence and found Penfold unmarked, the winger shooting wide. The Robins used Burder more than Cleland now, but the Welshman wasted a corner kick by putting the ball behind. McDonald also wasted a free-kick and Scott did the same with a corner. Cup tie nerves were probably to blame.

Reading were now faster on the ball and Gourlay was again called upon to save, this time from Whitehouse. The Robins were hard pressed to clear their lines and ten minutes after half-time McDonald was hurt when he was hit on the head by a shot from Cronin, but he was able to continue after treatment.

Hyde was playing the game of his life at centre-half for the Robins, saving them time after time. For about the fifth time in the match, Cleland was fouled. Farrel's kick was palmed by Meeson against the Reading crossbar and the ball was scrambled away. After defending for some time, the

Robins were now attacking and it was Reading's turn to defend. McAllister, however, found it difficult to beat Spiers, the Reading centre-half, especially in the air. Cleland gained corner after corner for the Robins. With lack of penetration in the middle, however, nothing resulted. More corners came to the Robins and first Meeson turned a header from Hyde over the bar and then McAllister shot wide.

After being penned in their own half for about ten minutes, Reading broke away and in the seventy-seventh minute, centre-forward Dixon headed in a cross from the left to give Reading the lead for the first time. The Robins did not really deserve to be 2–1 down, for they had more of the play than Reading. Their opponents however, had taken their chances better. Although with flagging spirits, the Robins fought for an equaliser. They were given two free-kicks near the Reading goal, but to no avail. The Robins kept up the pace and there were several anxious moments for Reading before the final whistle went, with Reading the winners by two goals to one.

Cheltenham finished fourth in the Southern League that season, behind champions Kettering Town, Bedford Town and Weymouth. Reading finishing thirteenth in Division Three South and, after beating Bedford Town in round two of the cup, they lost to Wrexham in a third round replay.

The total attendance was 8,326, beating the previous highest of 6,000 against Cardiff City.

Cheltenham Town: Gourlay, McDonald, Baird, Farrel, Hyde, Dunn, Cleland, Scott, McAllister, Keen, Burder.
Reading: Meeson, McLaren, Reeves, Anderton, Spiers, Evans, Penford, Whitehouse, Dixon, Cronin, Wheeler.
Referee: L. Callaghan (Merthyr Tydfil).
Attendance: 8,326.

MATCH 4: CHELTENHAM TOWN v. GRAVESEND & NORTHFLEET

Southern League Cup final, second leg
Saturday 19 April 1958, Whaddon Road
Cheltenham Town 2 (Cleland 23, Fowler 33)
Gravesend & Northfleet 1 (Thomas 75)

The 1950s brought a number of milestones in Cheltenham Town's history, including their one and only success in the Southern League Cup. The highest attendance ever to witness a match at Whaddon Road was recorded against Reading when 8,326 people saw the Robins lose 2–1 in 1957. Cheltenham's transfer record was broken with the club's first £1,000 signing, Matt Carson, two years later.

In April 1958, free-scoring Cheltenham defeated Gravesend and Northfleet over two legs to claim the League Cup. Cheltenham knocked out rivals Gloucester City 4–0 on aggregate in the first round before cruising past Bath City 7–0 in round two. The Bath mauling was the third time the prolific Robins had netted seven goals that season.

The Cheltenham squad that tasted glory in the Southern League Cup.

Hereford United and Guildford City were both ousted 2–1 in the quarter-finals and semi-finals respectively to set up a final against Gravesend, with the first leg at the Kent club's Stonebridge Road. With former Manchester City goalkeeper Bill Gourlay in fine form between the sticks, Cheltenham put themselves in a commanding position with a 2–0 success at Gravesend, who went on to win the Southern League Championship that season, while the Robins had to settle for sixth place, despite scoring 115 league goals – more than any other club. Goals from Peter Cleland and Jimmy Geddes had also earned Cheltenham a 2–0 win at Stonebridge Road in the league meeting between the two clubs.

A simple tactical move by manager Ron Lewin put the seal on the game and gave the Robins the chance of winning the Southern League Cup for the first time in the club's history. At least four of the Gravesend line-up were colleagues or opponents of Cheltenham's manager during the days when he was a full-back with Fulham. Moreover, he had watched Gravesend & Northfleet on one occasion that season when he analysed their strengths and weaknesses. He had a good cause for thinking that he could produce a plan for countering their attacking style.

It was perhaps a risk, but nevertheless one worth banking on, and the outcome was even better than Lewis dared hope for. Two goals, in the sixteenth and forty-sixth minute from Cleland and Dan Fowler respectively, added to the Robins' reputation as Gravesend's bogey team and sent 350 jubilant Cheltenham fans in the crowd of 3,162 on the way home full of confidence that their favourites could make sure of that coveted trophy in the second leg.

In the first leg the plan was simply to switch right winger Geddes and right-half Rex Dunlop, the object being to shut out Gravesend's sharp-shooting inside-left, Bob Thomas, who had scored thirty-two league and cup goals that season, and at the same time through Dunlop, exploit a gap in midfield caused by Thomas' unorthodox style as a twin centre-forward and goal-poacher. Geddes was practically Thomas' shadow for the entire ninety minutes and Dunlop had so much freedom on the right flank that he almost looked lonely. But perhaps as significant a factor behind Cheltenham's triumph was the Gravesend mud – almost ankle-deep in some parts of the pitch, which was covered in water five hours before the game began. This Cheltenham side was actually pleased to see rain for the Easter holiday. Their delight was evident right from the very start and they revelled in the mud. However, this bonus-earning victory was not obtained without a few anxious moments, during which Gourlay excelled himself.

The first was in the seventh minute when Thomas managed to give Geddes the slip and seemed certain to score with a right-foot drive from twelve yards, which Gourlay turned superbly round an upright. A minute later, Gravesend's best forward, Robinson, crossed for Day to head against a post with Gourlay well out of reach. Undisturbed by these escapes, the Robins started on the road to victory with a Clive Burder-made goal after sixteen minutes. He weaved round Carson and cunningly placed his centre out of the reach of Heathcote for the in-rushing Cleland to head home after Fowler had narrowly failed to connect.

It was indeed a cruel blow that the Fleet should have to face the second half with a ten-man team – Carson being off with a chest injury. Their disadvantage was emphasised after Fowler scored, but they made the kind of comeback which illustrated that Cheltenham could not afford to be complacent about their chances in the second leg. Shots from Day, Thomas and Logie took the paint off the woodwork and another inspired spell by Gourlay kept the visitors' goal intact. Late on, a drive from Day hit the underside of the crossbar and bounced on the line. Baird attempted to clear but booted the ball against an upright and Gourlay gratefully grasped the rebound.

Despite the frantic finish, Cheltenham won the second leg 2–1 to triumph 4–1 on aggregate. Cleland and Fowler were on target again at Whaddon Road, where Dunlop was presented with the cup by the president of the club, Sir George Dowty and nearly 5,000 fans were there to see it. Frank Carnie was presented with an individual trophy after playing in all the preceding rounds apart from the Gloucester City tie – only to suffer a leg injury three weeks before the final and put an end to his football for the 1957/58 season. It was a cruel blow because the talented young Scot would have liked nothing better than to have been in the thick of things when the Robins capped a wonderfully successful season by taking the cup for the first time.

Cheltenham get their hands on the Southern League Cup.

The match itself had everything – a wealth of good football, a captivating cup atmosphere and all the trimmings to suit the occasion. The Robins played as though they were two goals behind, not two in front, and their all-out effort was the key to capturing the silverware.

Cheltenham were masters right from the start and apart from a spell in the second half, they stayed that way. Man of the match Cleland led the home attack with such dash that he was an inspiration to the entire team.

Gravesend sorely missed forward Eric Day, who was injured. His deputy, Ron Walker, had a thoroughly unenviable time against Joe Hyde and long before the end he gave up the task, swapping places with left-half Bridge. Thomas did score for Gravesend in the seventy-fifth minute, but by that time the cup was Cheltenham's. The lethal pairing of Cleland and Fowler went on to score seventy-two between them by the end of the season.

Cheltenham reached the Southern League Cup final on two more occasions, losing out to Cambridge United 1–0 (1969) and Fisher Athletic 6–2 (1985) over two legs.

Cheltenham Town: Gourlay, Farrel, Baird, Dunlop, Hyde, Dunn, Geddes, Fowler, Cleland, Scott, Burder.
Gravesend & Northfleet: Heathcote, Thompson, MacDonald, Shaw, English, Bridge, Scarth, Logie, Walker, Thomas, Robertson.
Attendance: 4,900.

Match 5: Altrincham v. Cheltenham Town

FA Trophy First Round
Monday 22 January 1979, Moss Lane
Altrincham 1 (Rogers 60) Cheltenham Town 2 (Brown 1, 10)

Master poacher Dave Lewis was renowned for the goalscoring prowess that saw him net nearly 300 times for Cheltenham Town – a club record feat that is unlikely to be broken. However, it was at the other end of the pitch that he starred in this FA Trophy first round giant-killing act against holders Altrincham. Regular number one Jeff Miles was a building society manager in the Welsh town of Aberdare and was unable to take the time off work, but boss Denis Allen discovered that at lunchtime and was banking on Miles' understudy Nigel Berry turning up at Moss Lane. The squad set off for the north-west without a goalkeeper on board and Allen stopped the team bus just north of Birmingham to contact Berry, but it soon became apparent that he was not going to make it either. Lewis, who had already netted 247 goals in 405 starts in his more accustomed role for the Robins, donned the goalkeeper's jersey – along with a pair of baggy woollen tracksuit bottoms – for the first time in his life. With none other than legendary England World Cup-winning goalkeeper Gordon Banks watching on in disbelief from the stands, the twenty-six-year-old performed heroics to shut out one of the most formidable teams in non-league football at the time.

Southern League Premier Division Cheltenham went into the game without an away win in the league all season, but thanks to Lewis' heroics, they pulled off a major shock on a night full to the brim of traditional knockout romance. While Lewis somehow kept Altrincham out, Dennis Brown scored two wonderful goals in the first half to put Cheltenham on their way to a second round tie with Chorley. Altrincham were second in the Northern Premier League and had gone close to knocking Tottenham Hotspur out of the FA Cup ten days earlier, pocketing £35,000 from their two third round games against the top flight club before losing 3–0 in a replay. They tested Lewis for the first time in the opening minute, but an awkward free-kick from striker Graham Heathcoate bounced off Lewis' chest before being scooped up by him to safety in the most unorthodox fashion, as the tone for a frosty, but highly entertaining evening was set. The resulting corner was whisked up field to Brown, who was the only Cheltenham player in Altrincham's half. As goalkeeper Peter Eales left his line, Brown struck a left-foot shot early and from well out. Eales could only turn and watch it while it went on and nosed in off the far post.

Brown flattered to deceive during his time with Cheltenham, but his second goal of the night arrived in the tenth minute and was an absolute beauty. Graham Mackenzie, who had made a strong start to the match during Cheltenham's unexpected burst of fine attacking play, put John Davies away after a slip from Graham Tobin. Davies' touch to the left was sent searing past Eales from 25 yards by former Chelsea player Brown's trusty left foot.

One home fan standing behind the goal advised Lewis that he should be a centre-forward as he proceeded to volley away several other efforts in the first period. He dispelled any fears that he may not be able to cope with being the last line of defence in the thirty-fifth minute, plucking a headed effort out of the air as Cheltenham went into the dressing rooms two goals to the good. The man regarded as England's best ever goalkeeper, Banks, who was then assistant manager of Port Vale, remarked when asked about Lewis in the board room at half-time, 'Well, he's different isn't he!'

Brown had missed a chance to complete his hat-trick before half-time, but the second half was controlled by manager Tony Sanders' Altrincham from start to finish. Lewis was not the only player operating out of position. Two of Cheltenham's midfield four, Mike Coslett and Mark Payne, were not in their usual areas while Tim Bayliffe was in the unfamiliar role of left-back. Lewis continued to defy gravity amid an almost constant barrage, diving the wrong way on one occasion, but once again kicking the ball to safety. He threw himself at strikers' feet and despite standing only 5ft 5ins, he rose to push a long, dipping cross against the bar and it bounced back over the heads of two onrushing Altrincham players as the magic continued for Cheltenham.

Right: Dave Lewis in his more familiar attacking role for the Robins.

Below: Cheltenham's two-goal hero Dennis Brown.

Home skipper and the most uncompromising of players, John King, who had lifted the Trophy the previous season after his side had defeated Leatherhead 3–1 at Wembley, hit a post as it became clear that it was not going to be Altrincham's day. With half an hour to go, they did pull one goal back to set up a nervy finish for Cheltenham. Steve Foster gave away a free-kick when he fouled Barry Howard and was cautioned. From the resultant move John Rogers made it 2–1. The home crowd were lifted and Altrincham forced a succession of corners, but the eagerly anticipated leveller never arrived. Perhaps Lewis' finest save came in the eighty-seventh minute when Heathcote was presented with a free header eight yards out, but he anticipated where it was going to go, stopped it as he dived and gathered it at the second attempt. Ray Dean scrambled one off the line during injury time and the rest of Lewis' defence gave him brave protection in one of the most one-sided of halves as Cheltenham defeated their rival Robins.

Next, Cheltenham drew 2–2 at Chorley, where Lewis hit his 250th goal for the club. They won a replay 2–1 at Whaddon Road to reach the third round for the first time, where they crashed out 4–0 to the then mighty Enfield. Despite being remembered for his incredible goalscoring feats, when questioned, Lewis singles out this match as the one that stands out above all others as his most magical memory in a Cheltenham shirt. Who would have thought that shirt would have been green?

Altrincham: Eales, Allen, Brooke, Tobin, Owens, Davison, King, Heathcote, Johnson, Rogers, Howard (Crossley).
Cheltenham Town: Lewis, Murphy, Bayliffe, Coslett, Dean, Foster, McKenzie, Dangerfield, Payne, Davies, Brown.
Referee: P.B. Lancaster (Sutton Coldfield).
Attendance: 1,466.

Match 6: Cheltenham Town v. Gloucester City

FA Cup second qualifying round
Saturday 2 October 1982, Whaddon Road
Cheltenham Town 5 (Abbley 9, Dyer 30, Lewis 34, 75, Gough 82)
Gloucester City 1 (Williams)

Cheltenham Town found themselves in the unusual position of being a division below county rivals Gloucester City during the 1982/83 season. However, Southern League Midland Division Robins, managed by Alan Wood, had a chance to upset the Premier Division Tigers in an FA Cup second round qualifying clash at Whaddon Road. In 1982 the Southern League had been reorganised for the second time in four years. The previous structure of two parallel 'midland' and 'southern' divisions was altered by the reintroduction of a Premier Division. The top ten teams of each division were taken into the Premier, with the rest left to fight it out with new arrivals from the regional leagues. Cheltenham had been underachieving during the previous four years to such an extent that they found themselves two levels below what is now the Blue Square Premier Division (Conference) when the season kicked off.

They beat Thame United 3–2 in the first qualifying round, while Gloucester, who had been placed in the re-established Premier Division, overcame Llanelli in their opener. Gloucester arrived as something of an unknown quantity, with a series of new players who were unfamiliar to Cheltenham. Jimmy Gough, who had missed the Welsh Cup tie at Ebbw Vale a week earlier, was back hunting for more goals after bagging a brace against Thame. Stroud-born striker Paul Tester, who was later to move on to Shrewsbury Town, was fit again after a shoulder injury at Ebbw Vale, but was named as a substitute. Derek Bryant made way for Gough.

Six goals, five of them on the right side, one sending off and three bookings made it a highly eventful game as Gloucester were heavily beaten, leaving the Whaddon Road air thick with satisfaction. The damage was done in the thirty-seven minutes before the sending off of City midfielder Richie Overson for a foul on Norman Pemberton, who was forced off and replaced by Tester at half-time. Cheltenham's supremacy was signalled straight from kick-off when Gough was put clear by Dave Lewis, but the chance evaporated when Gough held the ball back and lost it. It started to become fact when in the ninth minute Steve Abbley anticipated and moved in on a careless back-pass by stop-gap central defender Dave Jones and swept it past City goalkeeper Mark Gwinnett.

Chris Ogden, rivalling Lewis as Cheltenham's player of the match, made an important save when he slapped away a volley by Gary Stirland, but City's defence had been lured into giving plenty of evidence of instability before the second goal came. The goal was credited to John Dyer, who cut in from the left and shot with his right foot. It hit Jones' leg and looped up, well over Gwinnett, in the thirtieth minute. Four minutes later it was all over bar the revival City were to make when they were down to ten players. Stuart Cornes jumped with Dave Bruton for an Abbley corner and got the nod and Lewis slid and volleyed in the third. With only thirty-four minutes gone it was beginning to look unbelievably easy, but once Overson had gone, Gloucester began to play their best football of the match. However, Ogden stopped everything except a shot from 30 yards by Mark Williams which dipped as it sped and looked a goal from the moment it left his foot. Just before, Ogden had beaten away a low drive by Ashley Griffiths. Lewis bundled in his second to make it 4–1 after Terry Paterson had done the work to produce a shot which Gwinnett had gone full-length to parry and Gough took time off from waving at the crowd to score the last, laid on by a through-the-middle pass from John Murphy in the eighty-second minute.

Gough was one of the players booked for shooting high behind the goal when he knew the whistle had gone and he asked for it. Earlier he had punched the ball out of Gwinnett's arms and also crashed into Gwinnett when he had little chance of reaching the ball. Jones of Gloucester was booked in the first half for knocking Abbley into touch and Steve Scarrott was cautioned in the second half for kicking the ball away – a harsh award. It was an occasion to savour for Cheltenham

Above: Paul Tester crosses.

Above right: Jimmy Gough.

Right: Steve Abbley gives chase.

and for ex-Robins Dave Hudd and Willie Ferns, who were there with Independent Insulations, whose sponsorship cheque was handed over before the kick-off. Wood said after the game, 'It was a good team performance and a good team result. We created a lot of chances and put them away and Chris Ogden made good saves at important times. It was a good game for spectators and give credit to Gloucester for not throwing in the towel.'

It was a successful season all around for Cheltenham, who went on to reach the fourth qualifying round, where they bowed out to Weymouth in a replay. They also reached the first round proper of the FA Trophy, the semi-finals of the Southern League Cup and the quarter-finals of the Welsh Cup, where they lost 3–2 at Wrexham. Most importantly, the Robins took the Midland Division title by one point from Sutton Coldfield Town. A 2–1 win over Oldbury Town assured promotion, leaving Cheltenham needing a point from their last game for the title. The visitors were Wellingborough Town, who made life very difficult in a very tense game. The final score was 0–0, enough to secure the Southern League Midland Division at the first attempt for boss Wood.

Cheltenham Town: Ogden, Dyer, Murphy, Cornes, Ryan, Paterson, Scarrott, Pemberton (Tester 46), Lewis, Gough, Abbley.
Attendance: 1,070.

Match 7: Cheltenham Town v. Alvechurch

Southern League Premier Division
Saturday 4 May 1985, Whaddon Road
Cheltenham Town 2 (Boyland, Hughes pen) Alvechurch 1 (Williams)

Cheltenham Town went into the final day of the 1984/85 campaign needing a point against Alvechurch to seal the Southern League championship and promotion to the Alliance Premier League for the first time in their history. The Robins, perhaps, should have sewn up the title weeks earlier, but with nearest rivals King's Lynn up against struggling AP Leamington, the pressure was on manager John Murphy's men at Whaddon Road. Murphy was dealt a blow in the build-up to the game as Ray Baverstock, whose tenacity in midfield had been a major part of the club's weaponry, was ruled out with an ankle injury. Paul Collicutt was suffering from bronchial pneumonia and lost half a stone in the run up to the match, but he was determined to play.

Murphy had schemed the club's surge in his first full season as boss, aided by two very important summer signings. He brought in established Southern League goal scorer Mark Boyland from Banbury United, while former Swindon Town and Torquay United midfielder Brian Hughes was persuaded to sign on the eve of the season. Hughes and Boyland scored fifty-eight goals between them in all competitions, Boyland weighing in with four hat-tricks. One of his treble came in a glorious 3–2 win over Gloucester City, helping send the Tigers down that season.

Other stars of the promotion success were wide men Nick Jordan and Steve Abbley, Hughes' midfield partner Ray Baverstock, central defenders Collicutt and Stuart Cornes and full-backs Clive Boxall and Steve Scarrott.

Goalkeeping howlers had cost Cheltenham in the latter part of the season, with Stewart Martyn, Tim Harris and Dave Mogg all playing well enough before finding themselves out of the side after losing matches which should not have been lost. They slipped up against Willenhall, at King's Lynn and against Fareham, their poorest performance of the season. If they had not, they could have clinched the title against Gloucester the previous Tuesday. Their goal difference going into the match was +41 in comparison to King's Lynn's +24. The next best in the division were RS Southampton with +25. Cheltenham had enjoyed a hugely successful season, reaching the final of the Southern League Cup and beating Gola League Weymouth on their own turf in the FA Trophy. They were unlucky to crash out of that competition at the hands of Bath City, another Gola League club and a high-flying one at that.

The Alvechurch game itself was a muddle, but the effect of the last whistle was amazing as Cheltenham 'got there'. Crowds surged forward to acclaim the players who had earned the club its biggest honour in fifty years. They sang, they stamped and they savoured the moment. They had won their first Southern League championship after surviving a horrific series of injuries and a staggering twelve games in the last twenty-five days of the season.

Even on the last day, fate did not cease to taunt them. Top scorer Boyland crushed his hands at work in the morning and played with a heavy bandaging on straightened fingers. Collicutt put out a shoulder again, becoming possibly the first skipper to receive the shield with an arm in a sling, days after being laid low with his bronchial illness. It was that sort of spirit that carried the team through the last couple of months and against Alvechurch, the struggles, worries and strains all became worthwhile. Despite his handicaps, Boyland still managed a goal, his thirty-first, in the twenty-second minute, a goal which helped to settle fraught nerves and which was wildly acclaimed by the 1,999 crowd. Cornes had already chased back 20 yards to kick one off the line, a Cornes clearance had smashed into Ian Ball and spun past a post and Alvechurch's Adrian O'Dowd had shot close. A suspicion of fraught nerves had been showing for a long time, but they were totally exposed by an Alvechurch goal by Mick Williams after fifty-nine minutes. A draw would have been enough for Cheltenham but Williams' goal filled every mind at the ground with visions of what might happen if Alvechurch scored another. They almost did; Scarrott kicked away from Gary Wright and Ball kicked off the line before Yeovil referee Brian Lock played a fateful hand. He pointed straight to the spot when Hughes, lying on the ground, kicked the ball into the air and it hit Malcolm Goodman's hand. Alvechurch went wild. O'Dowd was booked for dissent and Steve Howater was sent off for swearing at Mr Lock, to spark a four-minute hold up. There was jostling and argument near the Alvechurch dug out, but when it had quietened down, Hughes, with admirable cool, tucked away as vital a penalty as he had ever tucked away. Micky Brennan continued to complain and became the fourth Alvechurch player to be booked. Wright, in the first half, and Goodman were the others.

Chairman Arthur Hayward was unable to watch and he was pacing around Pittville Park when Player of the Year Hughes tucked away the penalty. Cheltenham survived the last eleven minutes and four minutes of time added on and the long, long trail had ended. Job done and a there was a new job to be undertaken in the top echelon of non-league football. After the game, Murphy said:

Brian Hughes is mobbed by his teammates after netting the goal that took Cheltenham into the Gola League.

It hasn't sunk in yet. I'm still thinking who's fit and who isn't and where the next game is. Saturday was such a nerve-wracking experience until 4.45 p.m., but we made it. I haven't found management difficult, but then I have only been doing it for a short space of time. The things I have tried to do all season have been my own ideas, although I have tried to learn from other managers I have played under. There's no magic wand or guarantees. In the end, it is the players; if you have good players, it is a matter of getting the best out of them. Getting promotion was the easy part. And now the hard work begins. I'm realistic enough to know where our weaknesses are. Certain positions need to be strengthened, but it doesn't mean that the person who has been playing in that position will be leaving.

Within an hour of the match Murphy was talking to a player he hoped might go into the Gola League with Cheltenham. Cheltenham won the Southern League Challenge match 3–2 against League Cup winners Fisher Athletic, who had beaten them 6–2 in the League Cup final. They were also victorious in their opening game at the higher level, winning 2–1 against Maidstone United through goals from Steve Brooks and Hughes. Murphy's men went on to finish eleventh in their first season in the Alliance Premier League, which was renamed the GM Vauxhall Conference for the 1986/87 campaign.

Cheltenham Town: Moss, Ball, Cornes, Collicutt, Scarrott, Abbley, Baverstock, Hughes, Boyland, Hacker, Jordan. Sub used: Goff.
Attendance: 1,999.

Cheltenham skipper Paul Collicutt is presented with the Southern League Shield.

Match 8: Wolves v. Cheltenham Town

FA Cup First Round
Saturday 14 November 1987, Molineux
Wolves 5 (Vaughan 23, Bull 27, 62, 83,
Downing 46)
Cheltenham Town 1 (Angell 20)

For three heady minutes, Cheltenham Town dared to lead at the home of Wolverhampton Wanderers in this FA Cup first round tie at Molineux. The only time Cheltenham had played Wolves prior to this cup encounter was a friendly to baptise the first floodlights at Whaddon Road in October 1951. Only Billy Wright of the then Wolves first team was not playing. It was just before Wolves' great era, but the Old Golds did feature Ron Flowers that day. Wolves were leading 3–1 with ten minutes to go when Cheltenham staged a rally which brought goals from Dean and Cowley. The first was a penalty by Rigby and Wolves' goals were scored by Neal, an own goal by Frank Allcock and by Roy Swinburne.

Of the Cheltenham team, at least four went on to play in the Football League – Frank Allcock and John McIlvenny with Bristol Rovers, Roy Shiner with Sheffield Wednesday and Hull City and Peter Rushworth with Leicester City. Their manager was George Summerbee, father of John, who played for Frampton United and of Mike, who played for Swindon Town, Manchester City and England.

At a dinner in the Plough Hotel after the friendly match, Cheltenham's chairman Keith Rushworth said, 'Perhaps we may meet again in the cup. Nothing would suit us better.' He did not realise he would have to wait thirty-six years for the privilege and the first ever competitive meeting between the two clubs.

And when Brett Angell scored a left-footed drive from 20 yards in the twentieth minute, hope sprang eternal for Conference club Cheltenham. It was as sweet a strike as you could wish to see and Angell demonstrated the sort of finishing skills that would later see him climb to the top flight with Everton. Angell was signed for Cheltenham Town by John Murphy as a raw nineteen-year-old in 1987 after spending two years on the books at Portsmouth. Angell responded by scoring twenty-five goals in thirty-nine games to kick-start his career before moving to top-flight club Derby County, managed by Arthur Cox, for £45,000 in February 1988. It was also a particularly big day for Mark Buckland, who went into the game nursing a groin problem. Buckland served Cheltenham as a teenager in the mid-1970s before moving to AP Leamington and then earning a dream move to Wolves in February 1984. He made his Wolves debut in the number two shirt in a goalless draw against Birmingham City. A week later he featured in a 1–1 draw with Manchester United at Molineux, but Wolves lost their top-flight status. He started at right-back, but the following season he played mainly in midfield and up front in Division Two. He scored his first Wolves goal in a 1–1 draw at Middlesbrough in September 1984 and his five goals that season made him joint top-scorer with Alan Ainscow. He was released at the end of that season owing to financial constraints and he linked up with Kidderminster Harriers of the Gola League. Buckland then returned to his hometown club, where he starred in a number of different positions and he had a chance to face his former club in this cup encounter.

In order to give themselves time for the most thorough possible preparations on their big day in the Black Country, Cheltenham had left Whaddon Road at 10.30 a.m., stopping at the Moat House for their pre-match meal in West Bromwich. They left the Moat House at 12.45 p.m. after a twenty-minute chat and arrived at Molineux at 1.30 p.m. The players' wives had their own coach and a third bore the club's directors and invited guests. Sponsors Duraflex provided new tracksuit tops to go with the normal strip of red shirts, white shorts and red socks.

Steve Brooks wins an aerial challenge with Wolves' Keith Downing who went on to manage Cheltenham.

Brett Angell celebrates his sensational opener at Molineux.

Cheltenham had already had to knock out Dorchester Town, Mangotsfield United, Weston-super-Mare and Bracknell Town to reach the first round. In the league, they had slumped to a 5–1 defeat by Lincoln City a fortnight earlier, but bounced back with a 2–0 success over Fisher Athletic to put them in a better frame of mind for their Wolves challenge. Unfortunately, dreams of a famous upset faded quickly when Nigel Vaughan rolled in Wolves' first goal three minutes after Angell's stunner. Manager Graham Turner's Wolves were unbeaten in eight matches and went into the game sitting on top of Barclays League Division Four (now League Two) on goal difference from Scarborough. They also had the highest average gate in their own league at that time, attracting 6,961 fans to Molineux. They were keen to avoid a repeat of the previous season, when they were embarrassed by non-leaguers Chorley, who won a first round, second replay 3–0 at Bolton Wanderers' Burnden Park.

Vaughan's goal was an untidy one for Cheltenham to concede. Richard Crowley could not prevent Bull getting a boot to a near-post throw by Andy Thompson, and Vaughan simply turned it in from in front. Four minutes after Vaughan's leveller, Steve Bull showed why he was taking the lower divisions by storm and justified his burgeoning reputation as a goal machine. The second was of a quality Cheltenham could not control. Bull, thirty yards out with his back to goal, turned and fended off Crowley's challenge before running beyond Kevin Willetts on the right of the box. The shot, lethally struck, flew away from Alan Churchward's groping right-hand and the delight of a few moments earlier had turned to despair for Cheltenham.

Glory hopes vanished just a minute into the second half, when Crowley and Willetts both failed to stop a surging run from Robbie Dennison. His ball inside was taken over by Keith Downing and the shot rolled beneath Churchward's dive. Downing was nicknamed 'Psycho' by Wolves fans as a result of his robust playing style in the centre of midfield. He joined Cheltenham as assistant to John Ward in 2004 and went on to manage the club between October 2007 and September 2008, helping them avoid the drop with a dramatic 2–1 win over Doncaster on the final day of the 2007/08 campaign.

Downing was not the only man in the Wolves side who would go on to manage Cheltenham. Former West Bromwich Albion stalwart Ally Robertson was then Wolves' club captain and he enjoyed back-to-back promotions under the management of Graham Turner and also captaining the side to the Football League Trophy at Wembley in 1988. Robertson was in charge of the Robins the season they suffered relegation from the Conference for the only time in their history in 1992, and he was replaced by Lindsay Parsons.

After Downing's strike, Churchward saved full length from Andy Mutch, Bull's strike partner, but after sixty-two minutes, Dennison and Jackie Gallagher combined and Gallagher's cross was headed strongly by Mutch. Churchward caught it, but dropped it when he realised he would probably carry it over the line as he fell. Bull needed no second bidding, and lashed in an angled fourth. Between then and the last, Bull's twentieth of the season seven minutes from the end, Wolves goalkeeper Mark Kendall made two desperate saves.

Wolves went on to beat Wigan Athletic 3–1 away in round two, but they lost to Bradford City 2–1 in the third round. Murphy resigned after a 3–0 FA Cup defeat by Gloucester City the following season, their first there since 1928/29. He was replaced by Jim Barron on 31 October 1988.

Cheltenham Town: Churchward, Buckland, Vircavs, Crowley, Willetts, Hughes, Baverstock, Brown, Brooks, Angell, Boyland. Subs used: Jordan, Townsend,
Referee: C. Downey (Hounslow).
Attendance: 10,541.

MATCH 9: BIRMINGHAM CITY V. CHELTENHAM TOWN

FA Cup First Round
Saturday 17 November 1990, St Andrews
Birmingham City 1 (Sturridge 57)
Cheltenham Town 0

Cheltenham may have bowed out of the FA Cup at St Andrew's, but they earned the respect of the Birmingham fans and staff alike after a gallant fight against their old Division Three (now League One) opponents. The Robins had defeated Exmouth Town, Weston-super-Mare, Worcester City, and Dorking en route to the competition proper. Their run through the qualifying rounds earned the club a rare chance to upset Football League opposition – something a Robins side had not achieved since they beat Carlisle United 2–1 at Brunton Park at the round two stage in the 1930s. Birmingham were managed by veteran campaigner Dave Mackay, formerly with Tottenham Hotspur and Derby County.

While Cheltenham had never progressed beyond round three, Birmingham had reached the final twice, although they had never won it in their 108 years since first entering the Football League as Small Heath Alliance. A bleak part of England's second city almost became the most beautiful place on earth for boss John Murphy's Cheltenham and the masses of supporters who witnessed their finest day for decades. They went closer to beating a club from the Football League than they had done since they held Watford to a goalless draw at Whaddon Road thirty years earlier, bombarding Birmingham's goal during the final ten frenetic minutes, but agonisingly failing to find a way through.

The Blues made a fast and furious start to the contest, putting the visitors under pressure from the first minute. Twice key man Nigel Gleghorn had teasing crosses from inside the box hacked away by Paul Brogan. Cheltenham's first effort came inside five minutes when Mick Tuohy headed Simon Brain's deep cross at goalkeeper Dean Williams. Cheltenham used former Wolves man Mark Buckland as a sweeper to combat the menace of Birmingham's front three. Despite the extra man at the back, however, Gleghorn caught the visitors out by sending Sturridge clear, but guest goalkeeper Steve Weaver had to move out of his area to clear. A chipped pass from Gleghorn caused panic and Dennis Bailey's header was cleared away by Buckland's knee, then Paul Tait missed his kick from eight yards when the ball bobbled his way.

Two errors from Birmingham in the space of five minutes could easily have seen Cheltenham take a two-goal lead. Matthewson miscued to let Kim Casey in, but Greg Downs came back to deny him inside the area. Then Williams charged down Simon Brain's shot after Vince Overson failed to look when attempting a back-pass. As the first half wore on, Cheltenham looked more and more comfortable and it was Birmingham who were looking edgy as the fans began to become impatient. Blues fans jeered their team off at half-time with chants of 'what a load of rubbish,' which was music to Cheltenham's ears.

It took the class pass of the match to break Cheltenham in the fifty-seventh minute and the man who scored, Simon Sturridge, was the only Blues player who had more speed than they could handle. The vision of £185,000 signing Gleghorn sparked the goal after Downs had dispossessed de Souza near his own penalty area. Gleghorn's sixty-yard pass from the left-back position caught Kevin Willetts absent and Sturridge beat Weaver with a brilliant finish to spare Birmingham's blushes.

Cheltenham had been faced with a goalkeeper crisis in the run-up to the game as regular number one Paul Barron quit the club. The Birmingham-based thirty-seven-year-old, who had earlier played for Crystal Palace and Arsenal, was a close friend of his namesake Jim Barron, who left the club a month before the tie after being told his contract was not going to be renewed. Recent signing Mike

Cheltenham salute their travelling fans after a brave performance at St Andrews.

Barrett, brought in by interim caretaker boss Dave Lewis, was cup-tied having played for Exmouth earlier in the competition, including their series of matches against Cheltenham in the opening qualifying round, which went to a second replay before the Robins triumphed 3–0 at Whaddon Road. That left YTS player Stuart Portlock, who was without a first team appearance to his name, as the only available goalkeeper on Cheltenham's books when the first round draw was made, but eighteen-year-old Weaver came in for the big game and acquitted himself particularly well.

After Sturridge's strike, Cheltenham did well to keep their shape and their heads, refusing to be intimidated. Casey was a big problem to the third division club with his pace and intelligent movement. In the first half he had cut inside Downs and John Frain before firing over the bar. In the second period, record signing Casey burst through, but failed to find the angle and, during the late onslaught, he volleyed fiercely and close.

Weaver made an excellent save to keep out a Gleghorn shot that had travelled through a sea of bodies following a short corner. However, Cheltenham finished the stronger and deserved at least a draw. They could take a great deal of pride from their effort as well as a hefty slice of the £36,000 gate receipts, netting half after expenses.

Mackay was quick to pay tribute to Cheltenham after the match, admitting they had given his side the fright of their lives and he also said he could not believe his side had held on to their slender lead at St Andrews after a 'scary' final ten minutes. While both sets of supporters united in a spontaneous tribute to Cheltenham, Lewis, who was now Murphy's assistant, was close to tears as he and the rest of the players went to salute their fans in the red and white corner of the ground. Lifelong Birmingham fan and season ticket holder Jimmy Brogan, brother of Robins player Paul, was among the hundreds who stayed on the terraces at the end to voice their appreciation for Cheltenham, who had been the very definition of the word gutsy.

Murphy resigned on 4 December, less than one month after rejoining the club for his second spell as manager. Midfielder Chris Burns earned a £20,000 move to Portsmouth in February 1991.

Birmingham City: Williams, Hopkins, Downs, Frain, Overson, Matthewson, Peer, Bailey (Gordon 81), Sturridge, Gleghorn, Tait. Sub not used: Fox.
Cheltenham Town: Weaver, de Souza (Crouch 73), Willetts, Brogan, Vircavs, Jordan, Burns, Brain, Casey, Buckland, Tuohy. Sub not used: Hancox.
Referee: K. Cooper (Mid-Glamorgan).
Attendance: 7,942.

MATCH 10: ST ALBANS V. CHELTENHAM TOWN

FA Cup First Round
Saturday 14 November 1992, Clarence Park
St Albans 1 (Duffield 56 pen)
Cheltenham Town 2 (Willetts 61 pen, Purdie 72)

Cheltenham Town held their nerve to see off in-form Isthmian League side St Albans and book themselves a home tie against AFC Bournemouth in the second round of the FA Cup. The right foot of Jon Purdie connected with a cross from Jimmy Smith on the left for the winning goal in the seventy-second minute of a magical match for the Robins on the perfect pitch which was used by England for training. Cheltenham then defied eighteen minutes of hell from St Albans before hitting the roof. They had put the club into the second round of the FA Cup for the first time since 1947/48 and they milked the moment.

Cheltenham's match-winner Jon Purdie.

Cup success and Cheltenham Town had not seen too much of each other over the years and the celebrations could not have been more joyous if they had been at Wembley Stadium itself. Bob Bloomer, veteran (at the age of only twenty-three), of 139 Football League games for Chesterfield, was the first into the crowd of ecstatic supporters and the last to leave, fists clenched in the air and dancing all the way back to the tunnel. They had taken on and beaten, in style, a team which had won every match at home and which had only lost two out of the twenty they had played that season. St Albans' reputation of being unusually good for the Premier Division, of what was then known as the Diadora League, was wiped away in the first half, when Cheltenham ran them ragged and tore to shreds any system they may have wanted to play.

Cheltenham's preparations had been hit by a series of injuries and striker Jason Eaton was cup-tied and unable to play. Lindsay Parsons played Neil Smith at sweeper behind Anton Vircavs and Steve Brown and between them they snuffed out the much-vaunted threat of twin strikers Steve Clark and Dean Williams. Only when St Albans got the ball out to Jimmy King, their outside left, did they look dangerous, and that did not happen often.

By half-time, tough-tackling and tireless Cheltenham had established a mastery they were not to concede. The best of the few shots was a first time effort from out on the left by Paul Hirons. It was tipped round the far post by Gary Westwood, but the finest times were yet to come. St Albans were given a penalty in the fifty-sixth minute, when two or three players closed on Martin Gurney as he went into the box. Wolverhampton referee Gurnam Singh ruled Andy Tucker's challenge illegal and Martin Duffield scored. It was totally against the run of play and three minutes later Cheltenham made a move which was to have a vital bearing on the game. Hirons was taken off and Purdie, not fit for ninety minutes, went on. His first touch brought another penalty, five minutes after St Albans'. He turned into the box, stopped abruptly, started again and had his ankle nicked by full-back Peter Risley. Kevin Willetts, calmness itself, drove it in and when Purdie slid in for what was to be the winner eleven minutes later, St Albans woke up. Then, and only then, did they look what they had been cracked up to be. They charged up the hill and charged again. Each time they were met by the unyielding wall of Vircavs, Brown, Neil Smith and anybody else who happened to be around. They defended heroically during that spell and suddenly they had achieved what no other Cheltenham team had achieved since before most of their parents were born. As soon as the final whistle blew, Cheltenham's players raced over to the goal behind which around 200 supporters had been chanting and cheering as hard as the players had played. Jubilant players mingled with supporters and sang songs late into the night.

The sixteen-man St Albans squad was on a £160,000 promise from a specially created insurance package, if they reached the third round, so their players lost not only the match, but £10,000 each as well. Robins boss Parsons said:

Getting into the second round for the first time in almost fifty years means more than £10,000. They're in the record book, and their names will go down in black and white. They're a young side and I'm proud of them from the oldest to the youngest. Kevin Willetts is the oldest and he said it was the best day he had had in eight years at the club. Andrew Tucker, at seventeen, is the youngest and he said it was the best day of his life. It was the best I have ever seen Anton Vircavs play, yet when he got on the coach, I truthfully didn't think he had any chance of playing at all because of his back injury. Jimmy Smith gave his best performance for the club. He didn't score, but he said he had never run as much in his life. Neil Smith and Steve Brown both had tremendous games at the back, and the attitude of Bob Bloomer, who has played more Football League games than any of them, has been superb.

Bloomer asked to play in the reserve team fixture the following Wednesday because he was blowing a bit after a suspension. Parsons continued, 'I think St Albans realised after the first five minutes that we were the better side. They watched us three times, but I didn't need to watch them more than once. The Cheltenham supporters were magnificent. They enjoyed their day and it carried on in the club when they got back. They have been good all season, but today they were different class.'

Anton Vircavs had an outstanding match in defence.

Peter Aitken, Parsons' assistant, said, 'Every player has given today what we have tried to instil from the start. They showed all the qualities needed to be a good side.' St Albans boss John Mitchell said:

From my point of view, we never got going. Whether that was to the credit of Cheltenham I wouldn't like to say, but it was our worst performance of the season. Cheltenham played very well and made it hard for us. I was disappointed by some of the things that happened for us, but I can't take anything away from Cheltenham. It was difficult for them to come here, but we ended up playing a long ball game and that's not our game. We never got any quality balls in to Steve Clark, and it is when you have balls coming across the six yard box that you suddenly start seeing him. Hand on heart, Cheltenham did it the nice way. It was nice to see them come and play very attractive football and Anton Vircavs had a superb game. He was my man of the match.

Parsons, who played over 500 games for Bristol Rovers during his playing days, built a fine footballing side during his time in the Whaddon Road hot seat. He guided the Robins to second-place finishes in the Southern League Premier Division three years in succession.

St Albans: Westwood, Smart (Brett 80), Risley (Scott 89), Downe, Price, Cockram, Duffield, Gurney, Clark, Williams, King.
Cheltenham Town: Nicholls, Howells, Willets, Brown, Vircavs, Tucker, Lovell, N. Smith, J. Smith, Bloomer, Hirons (Purdie 59).
Referee: G. Singh (Wolverhampton).
Attendance: 3,189.

MATCH 11: CHELTENHAM TOWN V. AFC BOURNEMOUTH

FA Cup Second Round (home) and replay (away)
Saturday 5 December 1992, Whaddon Road
Cheltenham Town 1 (Warren 83) AFC Bournemouth 1 (Shearer 12)

Youth trainee Christer Warren scored a dream equaliser against his hometown club to keep Cheltenham Town's hopes of causing a major FA Cup upset alive. It was almost fifty years since the Robins had defeated a Football League club in the Cup, but they went close to ousting Second Division club Bournemouth at Whaddon Road in the second round. The visit of the Cherries was the first home match against League opposition for Cheltenham since Third Division leaders Watford won 4–0 in 1968 in front of a crowd of nearly 5,000.

Matchday programme for the Robins v. the Cherries.

If eighteen-year-old Warren had not been named in the matchday thirteen, he would have been selling programmes in the car park as part of his duties as an apprentice. He was doing just that when Cheltenham were beaten 3–1 by Solihull Borough in the Beazer Homes League Premier Division in their previous match. Midfielder Simon Cooper, another Bournemouth boy on Cheltenham's books, was in the car park selling programmes. However, against the Cherries, Warren went on as a seventieth-minute substitute, replacing another youth trainee, seventeen-year-old home-grown talent Andy Tucker. Warren's eighty-third minute strike secured a 1–1 draw and earned them a replay at Dean Court, where they would be attempting to reach round three for the first time since 1933/34.

Warren had been subjected to jeers and chants of derision by the Whaddon Road crowd earlier in the season, prompting boss Lindsay Parsons to make a public plea to leave him alone. Against Bournemouth, he answered his critics. His goal, volleyed with his left foot, was his first at senior level. It was one of the fairy-tales that adorn the FA Cup. Warren was picked up playing for Ferndown Upper School against Cleeve School in the English Schools' FA competition and Bournemouth missed out.

Bournemouth, managed by Parsons' good friend Tony Pulis, were given a scare by Cheltenham as early as the first minute when Anton Vircavs' header flashed over the bar after Steve Brown had nodded on a corner, but that was to be Cheltenham's best moment until Warren set the ground alight. Bournemouth included goalkeeper Vince Bartram, who spent time on loan at Cheltenham at the start of the 1990/91 season, and midfielder Sean O'Driscoll, who went onto manage the club. He was only five matches away from claiming the club appearance record on 458. Winger Paul Hirons, who had scored against AFC Lymington and Worthing in the qualifying rounds, was ruled out with a back injury and it was his absence that opened the way for Warren to be on the bench. Cheltenham's Matt Lovell, aged nineteen, was a Bournemouth player until two months before the game, when he switched to Whaddon Road and he used to stay with Parsons at his Bristol home to cut down on the travelling to and from Bournemouth.

With so many connections between the clubs, there had to be a twist in the tale and the first came when Peter Shearer, sold to Bournemouth for £17,000 three years earlier, scored in the twelfth minute. It was a simple goal, chillingly headed at the far post as Keith Rowland's free-kick flew over Bob Bloomer and Shearer jumped as if Lee Howells was not there. Vircavs, Howells and Bournemouth's Alex Watson were all booked after a twenty-eighth-minute flare-up which started when Vircavs tackled Shearer. Three minutes before half-time, Kevin Willetts and Paul Wood made it five first-half cautions. Jimmy Smith scampered clear before rolling across a pass which did not reach Jon Purdie when he might have shot and right on half-time, Alan Nicholls made the best save of the game to turn away Adrian Pennock's shot.

If Bournemouth were expected to clamp down and govern the game after the break, then the expectation was misplaced. Instead, Cheltenham scurried about and Bartram fell on a free-kick by Purdie after Howells, having surged from his own half after robbing Shearer, was cynically blocked by Watson as he neared the box. Purdie curled another shot close to a post after Watson had knocked over Vircavs. All hope of a goal from either side had almost gone when Warren achieved instant stardom. He moved onto a short pass from Willetts on the left, brushed Purdie out of the way, and volleyed it low inside Bartram's right post. It raised the roof and raised a few Bournemouth temperatures too, and although nothing happened to make Cheltenham feel they could have won it, Bournemouth did nothing to suggest an upset might not have been on the cards in the replay.

Cheltenham Town: Nicholls, Howells, Willetts, Brown, Vircavs, Tucker (Warren 70), Lovell, N. Smith, J. Smith, Purdie, Bloomer. Sub not used: Wring.
AFC Bournemouth: Bartram, Pennock, Morrell, Morris, Watson, O'Driscoll, Wood, Shearer, McGorry, Morgan (Mundee 67), Rowland. Sub not used: Masters.
Referee: M. James (Horsham).
Attendance: 4,100.

Bob Bloomer on the attack at Whaddon Road.

Wednesday 16 December 1992, Dean Court
AFC Bournemouth 3 (Mundee, McGorry, Morgan) Cheltenham Town 0

Cheltenham travelled to Dorset for the replay knowing that a third-round tie at Blackburn's Ewood Park was at stake. Before the game, Cheltenham were rocked by news that goalkeeper Alan Nicholls, nineteen, had slammed in a written transfer request after being left out of a league match at VS Rugby for turning up late to two midweek training sessions. Nicholls tore up the request twenty-four hours later and was reinstated to the squad, but Alan Churchward was given the nod to start at Dean Court. Warren and Cooper had to be granted special permission to skip exams in order to make the trip to Bournemouth. They were both in the second year of a City and Guilds course in Recreation and Leisure.

Cheltenham gave everything they had and did themselves proud, but it was not enough and a powerful and clinical Bournemouth side progressed with a 3–0 win. Denny Mundee scored the opener in the eighteenth minute and Brian McGorry added number two in the seventy-third. There was no major difference between the sides after Mundee's opener and Jimmy Smith shot over after being played in by Lovell five minutes before half-time. Churchward made his best save, slithering across to his left post to turn around a shot by Morgan, just before McGorry's strike.

In the original match at Whaddon Road, goal hero Christer Warren takes the congratulations.

Cheltenham kept at it admirably before Churchward snatched at an unimpressive shot by Morgan and it twisted out and over the line as the Robins best FA Cup run for almost sixty years came to an end. At least 1,000 people from Cheltenham made the trip, almost filling the end set aside for them and they made as much, if not more, noise than the Bournemouth crowd.

AFC Bournemouth: Bartram, Pennock, Masters, Morris, Watson, McGorry, Wood, Shearer, Mundee, Morgan, O'Driscoll.
Cheltenham Town: Churchward, Howells, Willetts, Brown, Vircavs, Tucker, Lovell (Wring 81), N. Smith, J. Smith, Warren (Iddles 81), Bloomer.
Attendance: 5,100.

Match 12: Gloucester City v. Cheltenham Town

Beazer Homes League Premier Division
Monday 12 April 1993, Meadow Park
Gloucester City 1 (Penny 87)
Cheltenham Town 5 (Howells 7, Bloomer 40,
  Eaton 62, J. Smith 83 pen, Howells 87)

Cheltenham Town humiliated neighbours Gloucester City in front of their own supporters to make Easter 1993 a very happy one for Robins followers. Two players were sent off as tempers reached boiling point in the derby battle, but Lindsay Parsons' Cheltenham were streets ahead of their rivals, following up their 4–0 drubbing of the Tigers at Whaddon Road earlier in the season with an even more comfortable victory. Nothing is guaranteed to put a little colour into Cheltenham cheeks than the kind of embarrassment they inflicted on City at Meadow Park.

Parsons introduced a new strategy for the game and his plan worked perfectly. Both the previous full-backs, Matt Lovell and Paul Bloomfield, found themselves on the substitutes' bench, while back from suspension midfielder Neil Smith, converted striker Danny Iddles and Steve Brown made up a three-man defence. Bob Bloomer and Paul Hirons took position on the flanks and Steve Owen and Simon Cooper filled the midfield. Jason Eaton, who left Gloucester to join Cheltenham for £15,000 the previous October, played up front with Jimmy Smith, while Lee Howells spent most of the game charging forward and running the opposition ragged from a position just behind the front two. It was 5–0 before Gloucester scrambled their eighty-seventh-minute goal and Cheltenham scored two stretching their lead to 3–0 while they played for thirty minutes with ten men to City's eleven. They were a man light after the thirty-fifth minute sending off of Steve Owen for head-butting Shaun Penny at the end of a scuffle in which Ray Baverstock was also involved. Baverstock, no stranger to referees' notebooks when he was a Cheltenham player, was sent off himself after sixty-five minutes. He had already been cautioned when he threw the ball into Neil Smith's face and he had to go. Smith was cautioned as well and the incidents took away from some excellent goals, none better than the second, scored by Bloomer on the charge five minutes before half-time. His run started in his own half, and continued through an avenue of non-tackling City players before he cracked a ground shot past goalkeeper Russell Bowles into a corner. It was similar to a goal he had scored against Burton Albion the previous October. The versatile Bloomer had finished the 2–1 win over Halesowen Town in goal following an injury to Alan Nicholls, who had collided with a post in the thirty-sixth minute two days earlier.

It was probably the most significant goal of the match because Owen was off the field and Cheltenham had only the seventh-minute opener by Howells to cushion them. Howells, back after a three-match ban, played like a man possessed for the first twenty-five minutes and ghosted in for a visionary pass by Bloomer before cutting inside full-back Richard Criddle and scraping the ball beyond Bowles. A first-time shot by Jimmy Smith bounced off a post as Gloucester struggled to keep Cheltenham in check and apart from a long-range shot by Baverstock, and a drive past a post by Tony Cook, City's game was all defence.

Gloucester made a big effort in the second half and there were several scrambles on or around the Cheltenham line. Paul Hirons cleared from the line twice and later, a Tommy Callinan header hit the bar. However, they left themselves scarce at the back and Cheltenham's third, after sixty-two minutes, was headed in – just – off the underside of the crossbar by Eaton after Steve Brown had back headed on a corner. For a moment there was confusion as supporters and players scrambled to see the referee's decision. Mr Nocton of Rodborough signalled the ball had crossed the line for a goal.

Lee Howells is restrained by Tommy Callinan as Jason Eaton and Ray Baverstock look on.

Jimmy Smith scored the fourth from a penalty, given when Bowles caught him in the eighty-third minute and he was heavily involved in the fifth, when Howells put him away on the halfway line and kept going to meet the perfect cross.

Throughout the second half, Brian Godfrey's mid-table Gloucester had plugged away at reducing the deficit, their only tactic seeming to be an attempt to exploit the lack of height in the Robins' defence by lumping hopeful high balls into the box. City's goal was scored by Shaun Penny. Bloomer facing his own goal and not four yards away from it, was compromised and Penny's slithering shot rolled on after escaping Mike Barrett's second snatch.

It was Cheltenham's biggest Southern League win at Gloucester since they won 4–0 there on 13 April 1972. Cheltenham went on to finish as runners-up to Dover Athletic at the end of their first season back in the Southern League Premier Division, while Gloucester finished thirteenth.

Bloomer celebrates with Eaton.

Gloucester City: Bowles, Abbley (Fishlock 66), Criddle, Baverstock, Bywater, Kemp, Callinan, Penny, Bayliss, Cook, Noble. Sub not used: Crouch.
Cheltenham Town: Barrett, Bloomer, N. Smith, Brown, Howells, Owen, Cooper, Iddles, J. Smith (Lovell 89), Eaton (Bloomfield 74), Hirons.
Referee: B. Nocton (Rodborough).
Attendance: 1,072.

MATCH 13: CHELTENHAM TOWN V. CORBY TOWN

Beazer Homes League Premier Division
Saturday 27 August 1994, Whaddon Road
Cheltenham Town 8 (Howells 12, Boyle
 18, 51, 54, Smith 23, 40, 78, Eaton, 72)
Corby Town 0

Cheltenham amassed a club record 86 points during the 1994/95 campaign and Lindsay Parsons' men scored eighteen goals in their first five games to set an early pace at the top of the table. Eight of those goals came in a demolition of clueless Corby, who had problems on and off the field, but Cheltenham were in fine form and produced some of the most attractive football seen at Whaddon Road in years.

Corby had opened the season with a 1–1 draw against Trowbridge Town and a 5–1 defeat at Sudbury Town. Their defensive woes were to worsen at Cheltenham. Corby were one of only two teams to do the double over Cheltenham, along with Hastings Town, during the 1992/93 season, but on this occasion they were blown away by a rampant Robins side. Lindsay Parsons' men raced into a four-goal lead in the first half with goals from Lee Howells, Martin Boyle and a brace from Jimmy Smith as the frustrations of a 1–1 draw with Gresley Rovers four days earlier were taken out on the Steelmen.

Howells opened the scoring with a thumping shot from the edge of the box in the twelfth minute. Boyle, who had been recently recruited from Bath City for £6,000 made it two after a neat one-two with Smith, beating the 'keeper with a low shot and the Corby eighteen-yard box seemed to have been designated a tackle-free zone. Corby, whose record defeat was 9–0 against Merthyr Tydfil in 1978/79, lost veteran centre-half Gerry McElhinney, who had broken a rib in the Sudbury setback. The former Celtic, Bolton Wanderers, Plymouth Argyle and Peterborough defender said, 'I couldn't go on any longer. I knew it was broken, but I tried to pretend it wasn't. We had players out there who weren't being paid, and you can say the average was £30.'

The previous worst humiliation McElhinney had played in during his twenty-year career was a 7–1 beating when he was at Bolton and this was Corby's record Premier Division defeat. Their player situation was so dire that their first substitute, thirty-six-year-old David Barnett, was their reserve team manager and had only made one first team appearance before, on New Year's Day 1990. Eight players had walked out on Corby at the end of the previous season, following the departure of manager Elwyn Roberts to Nuneaton Borough. Former Nottingham Forest front player Calvin Plummer and long-serving Graham Archer followed him and Ian McInerney dropped into the United Counties League with Raunds Town. Free-scoring Anton Thomas went to Kettering Town and Mike Cook and Graham Retallick to Cambridge City. Another former Forest player, Bryn Gunn, in his third year at Corby, joined McElhinney as joint manager. Gunn was a former team mate of Cheltenham's Bob Bloomer at Chesterfield. Bloomer missed the game with a knee injury picked up against Gresley.

With McElhinney off the field, Corby were even more exposed at the back. Smith scored two identical goals in the twenty-third and fortieth minute, both involved latching on to a through ball and rounding the 'keeper to expose a static Corby defence. Boyle completed his hat-trick soon after the break with two quick goals in the fifty-first and fifty-fourth minute after more good work from Smith. Boyle and Smith formed an immediate understanding in attack at a time when Jason Eaton struggled to find a place in the starting line-up. Eaton entered the action in the sixty-first minute and it didn't take him long to find the net. Boyle turned provider, beating the full-back and crossing for

Left: Lee Howells and Jimmy Smith.

Right: Martin Boyle.

the arriving Eaton to shoot home from ten yards. All that remained was for Smith to complete his hat-trick in the seventy-eighth minute, finishing clinically after a strong run from Howells.

It was difficult not to feel sympathy for goalkeeper Paul Beresford, who must have felt like King Canute. To their credit, Corby refused to give up and Welsh international Martin Thomas, in the Cheltenham goal, was called upon to make some good saves late on.

The most goals Cheltenham ever scored in a match was nine, which they did in 1958, three times in a month! There were enough chances for that record to be broken, but they had to settle for eight. Perfectionist Parsons said, 'A couple of things were not quite right at the back. Back four players must keep their concentration and Martin Thomas had to make a couple of saves towards the end. Fair play to Corby. They didn't do what many other teams would do and lump it. They kept going to the end.' The win was Cheltenham's biggest since 1976 and Parsons' men followed it up with a 4–2 win at Atherstone and a 3–0 triumph at Sittingbourne. Jimmy Smith scored two in both matches to make it seven in three games for the diminutive Scot. They then beat a much-fancied Leek Town side 1–0 before meeting their match at Hednesford, losing 3–1. Hednesford, who included Mark 'Boka' Freeman in their squad, went on to take the title after a wonderful season which was too good even for Cheltenham's record-breaking squad.

Corby won only four league games all season, ending up bottom of the table. They shipped 113 goals in their forty-two league games and they also had a point deducted for fielding ineligible players. One of the highlights of their season was holding Cheltenham to a 2–2 draw in the return match at the Rockingham Triangle the following January, when goals from Neil Smith and Jimmy Smith were cancelled out by late strikes from Brett McNamara and David Hofbauer. Bloomer broke his leg in a collision with Martin Thomas and and Matt Lovell picked up a nasty knee injury to make matters worse for Cheltenham.

Cheltenham Town: Thomas, Tucker, Wring (Lovell 75), Banks, Jones, N. Smith, Howells, Cooper, J. Smith, Boyle, Mortimore (Eaton 61).
Corby Town: Beresford, Gould, Collins, Rayment, McElhinney (Barnett 17), Gunn, Ashdijan, Carter, Harrison, Oliver, Magrove (McLeod 54).
Referee: D.K. Curtis (Wotton-Under-Edge).
Attendance: 754.

MATCH 14: CHELTENHAM TOWN V. HASTINGS TOWN

Beazer Homes League Premier Division
Saturday 29 October 1994, Whaddon Road
Cheltenham Town 6 (Eaton 16, 59, 74, J. Smith 25, Cooper 34, Boyle 56)
Hastings Town 0

Cheltenham Town manager Lindsay Parsons once unwisely referred to Hastings Town as a 'pub side'. He was made to eat his words on several occasions as they earned a series of fine results against the Robins to become something of a bogey team during Cheltenham's five-year spell in the Southern League between 1992 and 1997. Newly-promoted Hastings recorded a win double over Cheltenham in the 1992/93 season and held them to a draw at the Pilot Field a year later, but Jason Eaton's goal earned the Robins a 1–0 victory at Whaddon Road in the return fixture. At the fifth attempt, Cheltenham finally made Hastings look like a bunch of Sunday League amateurs in this six-goal romp at Whaddon Road in October 1994. Eaton burst back to the goalscoring form which encouraged Cheltenham Town to pay £15,000 for him with a sharp-as-a-razor hat-trick.

Hastings 'keeper James Creed had been attracting interest from Football League clubs, but on this occasion, he spent most of the afternoon picking the ball out of his net. It was a good day for goals all around, but none of them would have been enjoyed as much as Simon Cooper's, slammed in from almost twenty-five yards on thirty-four minutes. Cooper was a tireless worker in the Cheltenham midfield, but he rarely scored goals. This one, when the ball looked to be running away from him, will always remain in his memory bank. It was Cheltenham's third and was probably the one that killed off hapless Hastings, who had conceded only seven in seven games before they leaked three in each half at Whaddon Road.

Their cumbersome defence could not cope with darting players like Eaton, Lee Howells and Jimmy Smith and the win took Cheltenham back to the top of the Beazer Homes League Premier Division, on goal difference from Hednesford Town. Even central defender Chris Banks attacked like a winger at one stage in the second half as Cheltenham showed their better face after their FA Cup failure at Bashley. Hastings had been a stubborn obstacle when they have played Cheltenham before during the previous two seasons and they had improved since Parsons' put down.

Cheltenham had put eight past Corby earlier in the season and the hint of goals was there early in this game when Eaton headed narrowly off target. A goal duly arrived after sixteen minutes when Hastings' Terry White tripped Jimmy Smith to give away a free-kick within shooting distance. Smith took it and his shot pierced the wall before bouncing off Creed's chest. Eaton reacted sharply with a crisp shot and nine minutes later he was involved in the second as well. Hastings defender Phil Henderson failed to cut out a long ball to the right and left Eaton free with Jimmy Smith in the middle. The obvious was achieved, with Eaton rolling his cross and Smith tucking it away. Cooper clouted his goal and after that, Cheltenham played with a freedom that had eluded them since the first half-dozen games of the season.

Martin Boyle, who had lifted one high and then headed wide at the far post, scored the next after Cooper had headed him clear in the fifty-sixth minute, and Eaton scored after Jimmy Smith had turned three players. Howells made the last by getting to the line and turning the ball back for Eaton and all in all, it was the sort of match Cheltenham's fans would be happy to watch every week. Only twenty-one days after this mauling, Cheltenham contrived to lose 3–1 at Hastings and their solitary goal was scored by a Hastings player.

Simon Cooper scored a stunner.

Jason Eaton netted a treble.

Cheltenham went twenty league games unbeaten between December and April, but still had to settle for second place in the Premier Division for a third year in succession, missing out on a return to the Conference to champions Hednesford Town. Hastings once again completed a double over Cheltenham during the 1995/96 campaign, reinforcing themselves as the Robins' bogey team. It was not until 1996/97 that Steve Cotterill's Cheltenham defeated Hastings twice in a season, 2–1 away and 1–0 at home, and they went on to claim second place in the league again, but this time it was enough for promotion to the Conference after a five-year absence.

Cheltenham Town: Thomas, Tucker, Bloomer, Banks, Jones, N. Smith, Howells (Warren 78), Cooper, J. Smith, Boyle, Eaton. Subs not used: Lovell, Cook.
Hastings Town: Creed, Ashworth, Willard, Henderson, Callaway, Powell (Smith 46), White, Wynter, Lovell, Playford, Barham (Lambert 58).
Referee: K. Pike (Gillingham, Dorset).
Attendance: 764.

MATCH 15: GLOUCESTER CITY V. CHELTENHAM TOWN

Beazer Homes League Premier Division
Saturday 26 December 1994, Meadow Park
Gloucester City 1 (Crowley 73)
Cheltenham Town 2 (Warren 46, Eaton 52)

Arch rivals Cheltenham Town and Gloucester City were both chasing Hednesford Town in a bid to win the Beazer Homes League Premier Division title when they met at Meadow Park on Boxing Day 1994. The match was given an extra edge by controversial pre-match comments made by Tigers manager John Murphy, who launched an astonishing verbal tirade towards his old club. Murphy broke off from plotting the downfall of the Robins to say of the club he took into the GM Vauxhall Conference, 'It's almost as if I was never there now. You usually feel that there is a special bond when you have been so close to a club, but after the passing of time, there is no affinity between me and Cheltenham now. They are always so hostile and suspicious and I haven't been to a game there since I left apart from taking Trowbridge Town there. I have to say that in six months at Gloucester I have been treated with more civility than I was in fifteen years with Cheltenham.' Murphy's five

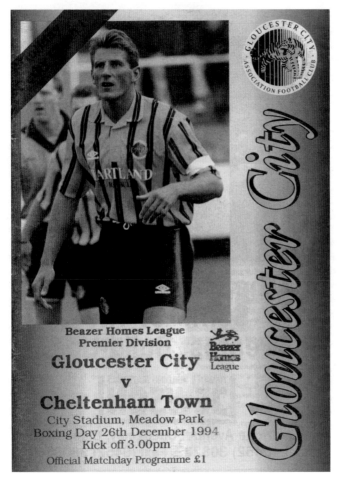

Gloucester City's matchday programme for the eagerly anticipated Boxing Day clash at Meadow Park.

years at Cheltenham ended after an FA Cup defeat at Gloucester in October 1988 and he talked about this decision in the run-up to the festive derby clash. He said:

I wasn't enjoying it. I'd been there a long time and things seemed to be drifting along almost. We'd lost a bit of sparkle and I was disappointed that we had sold so many good players and money to get new ones had dried up. Brett Angell will go down as one of the best centre-forwards Cheltenham ever had. He was in the England non-League squad by Christmas and I believe that with him, we would have won the league. A lot of good players there were not playing to the best of their ability and it came down to a choice. Either I moved good players on, or I tried something different myself. I regret going out of the Conference and if I had my time again, I would have stayed. But I had five years at Cheltenham and five years at Trowbridge and that teaches you that at this level, you have gone about as far as you can go in that time. It's very difficult to build a side over a long period because you don't know how long you have got to go. One thing I accepted more than anything when I came to Gloucester was that if I don't win the league in two seasons I will probably lose my job. I knew it would take me a while to get a team together, but people forget that at Trowbridge, we were in the Premier Division for three years and were top virtually all the first season. I needed more quality at Gloucester and it has taken us a while, but I am hoping in the next ten days to sign a left sided midfield player and a defender who can really finish the side off.

Arthur Hayward, the Cheltenham chairman who raised Murphy from the playing ranks after sacking Alan Wood said, 'I gave him his chance in football and I am disappointed if he feels he didn't get a fair crack of the whip.'

Murphy had built a strong squad at Gloucester, including several members who had followed him to Meadow Park from Trowbridge. Steve Portway, a feared goalscorer, was fit after recovering from a thigh strain, but David Webb was recovering from a broken leg. Cheltenham were without first-choice goalkeeper Martin Thomas, so on-loan youngster Neil Cutler was drafted in, on a wet and windy afternoon. Disappointing City had survived injury-hit Cheltenham's best efforts in the first half and the general expectation was that they would go on to win with the elements and the bulk of the 3,018 crowd behind them.

Football being the game that it is, the first few minutes of the second half made a nonsense of such thoughts and Cheltenham, with prolific striker Jimmy Smith playing in a defensive role on the left of midfield, surpassed themselves. Christer Warren scored the first during the opening minute of the half courtesy of a goalkeeping blunder by David Coles. Warren allowed a pass from Jason Eaton on the right to go past him before turning and striking a left-footed shot of no great power along the ground towards goal. Coles appeared not to see it until late, and when he dived, the ball rolled beneath his body. He should have stopped it easily enough, but it was a welcome break for Cheltenham.

The second, six minutes later, was of an altogether purer quality and in no small way due to a flash of skill by Jimmy Smith on the left. He turned full-back Alan Bird and made a few yards towards the line before curling over a delicate cross which Eaton met with his head four yards from goal. Coles blocked it, but the power on the header took it on and it ended up inside a post after a scramble of feet trying to keep it out. It was a sweet moment for Eaton, who quit Gloucester to join Cheltenham in 1992 and could always guarantee a hostile welcome when he returned to take on his former club.

Such events were hardly heralded during the first half, when Gloucester hardly raised a gallop and most of Cheltenham's shots were from outside the box and no great danger to Coles. Jimmy Smith almost caught him out in the early minutes with an outrageous lob from nearly forty yards. It had Coles scampering, but dropped the wrong side of his right post. It would have been a remarkable goal. Coles tipped over a drive by Martin Boyle and Jimmy Smith hooked close after the ball had bounced around in the box while Gloucester were still trying to find their bearings. Their first chance was in the twenty-sixth minute when Mark Hallam moved in well for a cross by Kevin Willetts, but got too far underneath it and the header went almost vertically over the bar.

Christer Warren opened the scoring with some help from City goalkeeper David Coles.

Cheltenham continued to call the tune and City only sporadically looked a side who had crept into the top three. Warren could have killed it off in the sixty-first minute when Bird slipped to leave him clear to bear down on Coles in a thirty-yard run which ended with Coles getting a hand to the shot. City hardly showed until Portway and Aidy Harris went on as substitutes and they pulled one back in the seventy-third minute. Former Cheltenham defender Richard Crowley scored it after Portway had headed against the bar from a corner which goalkeeper Cutler slapped to him. Cutler was to distinguish himself when he clutched a strong header by Portway on his line in the last minute and there was still time for him to use his 6ft 4ins to punch away another corner when City were thronging in the box.

Cheltenham and Gloucester had played each other fifty-seven times in the previous forty-seven years and Cheltenham claimed their thirty-third win. City had won only nine. After the match, Murphy said:

We never really got going. Hallam had a good chance, but the wind was probably the major factor. We all felt at half-time that we would be able to step up our game, but it didn't turn out that way. The early goal knocked us out of our stride and it was almost as though the sides cancelled each other out. In the end, Cheltenham deserved to win. They defended more resolutely and were quite strong on the break.' A delighted Lindsay Parsons said, 'I was really proud of my players. Everybody knows we have had lots of injuries, but in spite of them and the difficult weather conditions, we didn't have one bad player out there. We always seem to perform better when we are the underdogs.

Gloucester City: Coles, Bird, Willetts, Kemp (Portway 58), Kilgour, Crowley, Knight, Shearer (Harris 68), Hallam, Adebowale, Mitchell.

Cheltenham Town: Cutler, Jones, Bloomer, Banks, N. Smith, Cooper, Wring, Warren, J. Smith, Boyle, Eaton. Subs not used: Mortimore, Howells, Cook.

Referee: B. Baker (Andover).

Attendance: 3,018.

MATCH 16: CHELTENHAM TOWN V. HEDNESFORD TOWN

Beazer Homes League Premier Division
Saturday 11 March 1995, Whaddon Road
Cheltenham Town 2 (Boyle 6, Smith 52)
Hednesford Town 0

The Robins were battling to win promotion back to the GM Vauxhall Conference from the Beazer Homes League Premier Division at the third attempt and they met their main title rivals in a crunch clash at a very wet Whaddon Road. Hednesford Town were enjoying an impressive campaign and had already beaten Cheltenham 3–1 at their Cross Keys ground earlier in the season. They had only been beaten twice in twenty-nine games and included in their line-up imposing central defender Mark Freeman, who was later to become a Cheltenham legend as well as Joey O'Connor, the hottest striking property outside of the Conference.

A bumper crowd of 2,031 – their highest in over a year – assembled and Cheltenham needed a win to put pressure on their opponents, who were threatening to run away with the championship and had been brushing aside teams with ease. Full-backs Bob Bloomer and Matt Lovell were both ruled out with long-term injuries picked up in a 2–2 draw at Corby Town two months earlier.

Manager Lindsay Parsons had fired up his side and Cheltenham came out with all guns blazing. Christer Warren's header on at the near post set up Martin Boyle and his instant volley flashed just past an upright. Just once, after only forty seconds, did the Pitmen cause disarray in Cheltenham's defence, as O'Connor elbowed himself goalside of Steve Jones and shot on the run, but the ball was not fully under his control and went wide. After a series of early attacks at the other end, the Robins were rewarded with a sixth-minute breakthrough. Jimmy Smith's corner was only cleared to the edge of the penalty area and the ball fell to Boyle. After seeing his initial effort blocked by a defender, the forward calmly placed the ball into the bottom corner to give Cheltenham the early initiative.

With so much at stake, both sides were fully committed in every tackle and some over-exuberant challenges on a mudbath of a pitch resulted in four bookings inside the first fifteen minutes, including Freeman and Steve Devine. The game boiled over after twenty-eight minutes when Hednesford full-back Kevin Collins was dismissed after an altercation with Simon Cooper. A punch appeared to have been thrown as the players wrestled on the ground.

Cheltenham had won their previous six home league games and they produced some grand, flowing football despite the muddy conditions. The defence, marshalled by man-of-the-match Chris Banks kept dangerman O'Connor unusually quiet. The Pitmen did show glimpses of their quality, but never really threatened Martin Thomas' goal and Neil Smith and Cooper came close to extending Cheltenham's lead before the break.

Robins skipper Neil Smith sustained a cut to his face in the opening minutes of the second half and the midfielder typified Cheltenham's spirit when he had to be virtually dragged off the pitch, such was his desire to continue in the engine room. His main concern was whether he would be able to find some padding to wear over his eye that would allow him to play in the following fixture against Dorchester Town. He was replaced by Jimmy Wring as Cheltenham started the second period strongly and doubled their lead after fifty-two minutes. Banks picked up the ball on the edge of his own area and set off on a mazy run that took him all the way to the edge of the opposition area, where he was tripped. Lee Howells touched the resulting free-kick to Jimmy Smith, who curled a majestic shot into the top corner to raise the Whaddon Road roof. It was a repeat of the one which the Scotsman had pulled off the previous month against Halesowen Town. Cheltenham were then

Jimmy Smith.

Neil Smith.

content to sit back and soak up some pressure from the visitors and hit them on the break using the pace of Warren, who ran himself into the ground. Exciting talent Warren was to earn a big money move to top flight club Southampton before the season was out.

Banks made a superb challenge on Brendan Hackett as the striker shaped to shoot for goal, while at the other end the indefatigable Cooper and Wring were denied by Hednesford 'keeper Paul Hayward. No more goals followed and the memorable win meant that Cheltenham could have been top of the league by the end of the week. The victory over the team the rest of the division was chasing, along with a 4–1 win at Gresley Rovers four days earlier, meant Cheltenham had pulled back six of the eleven points by which Hednesford were leading by at the start of the week. Parsons was proud of his team, whom he said were superior to Hednesford all over the pitch, while Hednesford boss John Baldwin, who had led his side into the Premier Division in 1992, was unhappy about the refereeing decisions that had gone against his side as his side picked up several yellow cards as well as Collins' dismissal.

A great day for Cheltenham was made complete by their bitter rivals and another of the title contenders, Gloucester City, going down 2–1 to Hastings Town. It left the Tigers level on points with Cheltenham, but they had played three games more. After back-to-back runners-up finishes behind Dover Athletic and Farnborough Town, the title was in Cheltenham's hands with fourteen games remaining, but once again they had to settle for second best as Hednesford recovered from this setback to storm to the title by a margin of seven points, finishing on an impressive ninety-three.

Cheltenham Town: Thomas, Benton (Eaton 79), Howell, Banks, Jones, N. Smith (Wring 48), Howells, Cooper, J. Smith, Boyle, Warren. Sub not used: Cook
Hednesford Town: Hayward, Yates, Collins, Freeman (Street 60), Essex, Carty, Fitzpatrick, Devine, Hackett (Simpson 69), Burr, O'Connor.
Referee: P.R. Sharpe (New Barnet).
Attendance: 2,031

Match 17: Gloucester City v. Cheltenham Town

**Beazer Homes League Premier Division
Monday 8 April 1996, The City Stadium,
 Meadow Park
Gloucester City 0
Cheltenham Town 3 (Eaton 56, 74, Elsey 73)**

A fine performance from manager Chris Robinson's new-look Cheltenham side earned the Robins a fourth consecutive win at Gloucester's Meadow Park in another Easter Monday romp. Cheltenham followed up 5–1, 3–1 and 2–1 wins with a comfortable 3–0 victory against their yellow and black rivals to give their fans something to celebrate towards the end of a transitional season. Rushden & Diamonds and Halesowen had already pulled away at the top of the table, but third place was still up for grabs and there was plenty of local pride to be played for.

Cheltenham started their Easter Bank Holiday with a 1–0 home win over Merthyr Tydfil, with Jimmy Wring netting the decisive goal in the fifty-third minute. They had beaten Gloucester 3–1 on penalties in the final of the Gloucestershire Senior Cup only six days earlier after a goalless draw at Whaddon Road. It was the second year in succession the Senior Cup had been won by Cheltenham on spot kicks – they defeated Yate Town in 1995. The previous league meeting between the two sides had also ended 0–0 on 27 February, having been postponed on Boxing Day because of a frozen pitch.

Gloucester included former Robins Ian Howell and Simon Cooper. Striker Jason Eaton, who made the move along the A40 in the opposite direction up to Cheltenham in 1992, had scored at least one goal on every return visit to his former club and he kept up his remarkable record with a brace of second-half goals. The first half was fairly even but Cheltenham dominated the second period and only some fine goalkeeping from City 'keeper David Coles kept the score down. Eaton opened the scoring ten minutes after half-time, after good work from Jimmy Smith on the right wing. Smith bamboozled Tigers' left-back David Johnson and crossed for his partner in crime to finish from close range. Two goals in as many minutes followed, the first a well struck volley from David Elsey after a half clearance had fallen to him. Eaton then delicately beat Coles again to make it three after some more fine wing play from Smith, who proved that he could provide as well as score goals himself.

Cheltenham 'keeper Kevin Maloy made two important saves as Gloucester attempted to salvage some pride. Maloy was the sixth goalkeeper used by the Robins that season after Martin Thomas, Mark Teasdale, Shane Cook, Mark Davis and Nick Goodwin.

Chris Banks had a goal disallowed and Eaton was denied a hat-trick by Coles' agility as memories of the glorious five-goal romp of 1992/93 came flooding back. Defender Elsey was shown a red card after two cautions but that could not dampen the Cheltenham spirits as once again they showed their superiority over their big-spending neighbours. Robinson's side went on to finish third, twenty points behind champions Rushden, and although the Robins boss was sacked the following season, some of the foundations for the future years of glory had already been laid. Both Cheltenham and Gloucester had been actively rebuilding their squads and this match demonstrated the Robins were a few months ahead of the men in yellow and black and signs for the next season were beginning to look encouraging. Mark Freeman and Chris Banks were together at the back and with Bob Bloomer in the engine room and Eaton and Smith up front, Cheltenham were looking like a side ready to take on the non-league elite in the Conference. They just needed the right man at the helm and that man was to arrive the following winter in the shape of Steve Cotterill. After the game, Eaton said:

Jason Eaton was the scourge of Gloucester once again.

David Elsey saw red for Cheltenham.

Kevin Maloy made a fine stop late on.

The harder you work, the more chances come to you. I feel my overall game is going quite well at the moment. I thought I was unlucky against Merthyr on Saturday when I could have had a couple of goals. I obviously took my frustrations out on Gloucester! I don't know what it is – perhaps it's the understanding between me and Jimmy Smith. We've been playing together for most of the season now and I can read him quite well and he can read me. You need a good run in the side. It is a confidence thing. I still think I am an unlucky player. People have said a lot of things about the side and the players we have now, but I think we are a strong side and a settled side myself and I can't wait for Saturday to get on the score sheet again.

Up to that point, Eaton had netted twenty-one goals during the 1995/96 season, six of them in the last seven games. He finished with twenty-four goals, taking the Manager's, Players' and Supporters' Player of the Year awards.

Gloucester City: Coles, Holloway (Howell 20), Johnson, Thorne, Kemp, Rouse (Vernon 61), Webb, Adebowale, Cooper (Milsom 64), Black, Mardenborough.
Cheltenham Town: Maloy, Wotton, Benton (Campbell 87), Banks, Freeman, Elsey, Bloomer, Wring, Eaton, Smith, Chenoweth (Wright 74). Sub not used: Parker.
Referee: I.C. Mills (Kidlington).
Attendance: 1,523

Match 18: Cheltenham Town v. Bath City

FA Cup Fourth Round Qualifying replay
Tuesday 29 October 1996, Whaddon Road
Cheltenham Town 4 (Boyle 90, Eaton 91, Smith 93, Howells 110)
Bath City 1 (Davis 35)

Cheltenham Town were seconds away from being knocked out of the FA Cup at the fourth qualifying stage before a truly emphatic comeback pulled the plug on Bath City at Whaddon Road in 1996. Following wins over Gosport Borough, Salisbury City and Weymouth, Cheltenham Town were drawn away at struggling Conference club Bath in the final round before the competition proper. The Robins, managed by Chris Robinson, battled to earn a goalless draw at Twerton Park in the first match to bring the Romans back to their home for another crack at the Conference's bottom club. It was a hard-fought game played at a fair pace and the 0–0 scoreline was not a reflection of the number of chances created. Both sides could have won the game comfortably, with Bath hitting the bar and Cheltenham's Dean Clarke hitting the post with an angled shot. Both goalkeepers made good saves and there were moments of frantic penalty box action. Premiership referee Paul Durkin ruled the game with an iron fist and six players were booked. With twenty minutes to go, defender Eddie Murray was sent off after an incident involving Lee Howells. However, the Bath team worked extremely hard to overcome the loss in numbers. A draw was probably a fair result, but Cheltenham were disappointed not to have beaten goalkeeper Mark Hervin at least once considering the amount of possession they had. Hervin was making his first appearance of the season, former Robins number one Dave Mogg having played in each of their first nineteen games of the campaign.

The clubs' first FA Cup meeting was at the same stage of the 1937/38 season, when Cheltenham won 4–1 and they were to repeat that scoreline in what was to be an epic replay. Cheltenham had numerous early chances, but Mike Davis put Bath ahead after thirty-five minutes. Bath, who included former Robin Richard Crowley, defended stoutly and despite long periods of pressure, Cheltenham could not find a breakthrough.

Bath had a good FA Cup pedigree having knocked out eight Football League clubs over the years compared to Cheltenham's one. The Robins had been knocked out of the Cup by the Romans, on their way to a second-round tie against Stoke City, after a replay in 1993/94 and history looked set to repeat itself. Many home fans had already given up hope and left the ground when Kevin Maloy launched an injury time free-kick long into the Bath half. Substitute Martin Boyle, who had gone on in place of defender Mark Freeman in the sixty-seventh minute to add presence to the attack, stooped to head home a dramatic equaliser against his former club and it was then that the magic began. Bath were visibly deflated by the last-gasp leveller and Cheltenham capitalised with two goals in the first three minutes of a memorable extra-time period for the Robins faithful. With a tie against Barry Fry's League One outfit Peterborough at stake in the first round, Cheltenham ran riot. Jason Eaton, who hit a hat-trick in the 4–3 Second Qualifying Round win over Salisbury, received the ball with his back to goal on the penalty spot, turned sharply and drilled home Cheltenham's second. Barely two minutes later, Jimmy Smith scored a breath-taking third, lobbing the ball over Bath 'keeper Mark Hervin from twenty-five yards, out on the left side of the pitch, after exchanging passes with Boyle.

The tie settled down after Smith's wonder goal but there was just enough time for Lee Howells to crash a shot into the roof of the net in the second period of extra-time to make the scoreline even

Left to right:
Martin Boyle,
Lee Howells,
Bob Bloomer,
Darren Wright and
Jason Eaton.

more impressive. Cheltenham's FA Cup record before Steve Cotterill arrived was average to say the least, but this was a rare Cup night when it was great to be a Cheltenham Town supporter. Boss Robinson predicted that his side's sensational recovery would be worth £20,000 to the club. He said, 'We deserved it. We could have sewn it up in the first twenty minutes. It was just like that in the first match at Bath when we outplayed them and couldn't score. My message to the players when it was 1–1 after ninety minutes was "Keep the faith." I told them to trust in the ability of our players. We have good forwards and they will score, and they did.' Robinson's side went to Peterborough's London Road ground and held out for a 0–0 draw. The Posh dominated, but Jamie Victory headed against a post in the dying minutes. The replay saw a Peterborough side in dire financial trouble win 3–1, after extra-time.

Mark Freeman on the run for Cheltenham.

Cheltenham Town: Maloy, Wotton, Wring, Banks, Freeman (Boyle 67), Victory, Howells, Wright, Eaton, Smith, Clarke (Bloomer 100). Sub not used: Gannaway.
Bath City: Hervin, Murray, Dicks, Cross, Crowley (Harrington 100), Honor, Brooks, James (Tovey 60), Davis (Withey 76), Adock, Wyatt.
Referee: S. Dunn (Bristol)
Attendance: 1,018.

FA Cup First Round
Saturday 16 November 1996, London Road
Peterborough United 0 Cheltenham Town 0

Boss Chris Robinson's Cheltenham travelled to London Road to take on Division Two strugglers Peterborough United, managed by Barry Fry, in the First Round of the FA Cup. After a memorable 4–1 victory over Conference side Bath City in the final qualifying round, Southern League Cheltenham were full of confidence and Posh were in the midst of financial turmoil. Fry had already announced that he was to become the owner of Peterborough before Christmas, with the club £2.5 million in debt. Despite the contrasting fortunes on and off the pitch, there was still a huge gulf between the two teams and Cheltenham expected to be up against it as kick-off approached.

Fry sprung a selection surprise by recalling right-back Adrian Boothroyd to the side. Goalkeeper Jon Sheffield was also back in the side after missing the previous week's defeat at Walsall through illness. The Robins were given a boost before the game as influential defender Chris Banks was given the all-clear to play after recovering from an injury.

Peterborough included former Cheltenham midfielder Derek Payne in their starting line-up alongside Captain Martin O'Connor who was being watched closely by Birmingham after some impressive performances for Posh. Blues boss Trevor Francis was in the crowd, along with former Cheltenham manager Jim Barron. Injured defenders Steve Benton and David Elsey joined Robins supporters in the terracing behind the goal, joining in with the singing and chanting to help their team-mates achieve a favourable result.

The home side took control immediately and found plenty of space to stroke the ball around, with Cheltenham content to sit back and soak up pressure with the hope of hitting back on the counter attack. Cheltenham were given a huge first-half let-off when O'Connor dragged a penalty kick wide of Kevin Maloy's right-hand post. The spot kick had been awarded for a trip on Scott Houghton by Banks, who was adamant the penalty should not have been given in the first place. After the miss, Cheltenham noticeably grew in confidence and began to show composure and determination that would become a feature of their game for the remainder of the season. They battled for every ball and held a good defensive shape to frustrate their full-time opponents. In the forty-second minute, Jimmy Smith had a chance after a mix-up between Sheffield and Greg Heald, who were trying to deal with a cross from Banks, but Smith failed to generate any power with his shot and Mick Bodley was able to get across to divert it around the post.

Mark Freeman relished the physical challenge posed by Ken Charley, and Jamie Victory made progress on the left flank as Cheltenham began to find their feet and play some football of their own. Freeman made Sheffield fly to tip over a twenty-yard drive. Peterborough looked like a decent side but morale was clearly low and as chances went begging, Cheltenham looked more and more capable of causing an upset. As the final whistle grew near, Victory rose majestically to meet a Lee Howells corner with his head, only to see the ball rebound back off the post. Kevin Maloy only had to make one real save during the ninety minutes. Charley forced it when he burst into the box on the right side, but Maloy's positioning was just right and he twisted to beat the drive round a post after sixty-five minutes. Freeman felled Charley in the penalty box and got away with it four minutes later, a decision which brought huge howls from the Peterborough fans.

Cheltenham maintained their composure and the game finished goalless, sparking the jubilant Robins' unique celebrations. In response to comments made in the local press that claimed striker Smith possessed the physical presence of 'Larry the Lamb', the entire team got down on all fours and in the style of sheep made their way into the goal in front of their army of 1,000 travelling fans. Prolific Scotsman Smith worked part-time behind the bar in Cheltenham's social club at the time. It was only the third time in their long history that Cheltenham had played on a Football League ground in the FA Cup and not lost.

Highlights of the replay were shown on BBC's *Sportsnight* and generated some valuable funds for both clubs. A crowd of over 4,000 assembled at Whaddon Road to see Cheltenham once again push Peterborough all the way. Fry's men scored three in extra-time through Ken Charley (2) and Giuliano Grazioli, leaving Jimmy Smith's 116th-minute penalty, after Bob Bloomer was tripped, as scant consolation. Charley's opener came after a header from Banks back to Maloy fell short, allowing the striker to steal in and deflate Whaddon Road. In normal time, Sheffield had made a full stretch save to deny Lee

Chris Banks holds off former Cheltenham midfielder Derek Payne.

Howells. Despite the result, it was still a wonderful occasion as Cheltenham came as close as they had done to defeating Football League opposition since Carlisle United were knocked out sixty-three years earlier.

The BBC brought around 1,000 extra lux with them to improve the lighting for the Posh clash and the packed ground looked superb on TV, with Howells named man-of-the-match for a typically dynamic midfield display. The crowd of 4,160 was the highest attendance at Whaddon Road since 1951, when 5,000 packed in to see a 3–3 draw with Wolves in the first ever floodlit match.

Cheltenham go wild in the dressing room at London Road after their fine draw against the Posh.

Peterborough United: Sheffield, Boothroyd, Clark, O'Connor, Heald, Bodley, Willis (Carter 58, Ebdon 89), Payne, Rowe (Grazioli 52), Charley, Houghton.
Cheltenham Town: Maloy, Wotton (Bloomer 89), Wring, Banks, Freeman, Victory, Freeman, Howells, Wright, Boyle (Eaton 57), Smith (Chenoweth 90), Clarke.
Referee: M.E. Pierce (Portsmouth)
Attendance: 5,271.

Match 20: Halesowen Town v. Cheltenham Town

Dr Marten's League Premier Division
Saturday 29 March 1997, The Grove
Halesowen Town 1 (Freeman og 31)
Cheltenham Town 5 (Knight 60,
  Dunwell 73, 75 pen, Wright 81, Boyle 87)

MAIN SPONSOR:

Hamer Ford

Halesowen Town F.C.
V
Cheltenham Town

Saturday 29th March 1997
Kick Off. 3.00pm

£1.00

Two days before their Easter Monday Dr Marten's Premier League promotion showdown with bitter local rivals Gloucester City at Whaddon Road, Cheltenham faced a tricky-looking trip to Halesowen Town. The fourth-placed Yeltz were always difficult opponents, especially on their own turf, but Cheltenham had emerged victorious in the sides' previous meeting at Whaddon Road. That match marked Steve Cotterill's first win as Cheltenham boss, ex-Halesowen man Keith Knight scoring at both ends as the Robins won 2–1.

Halesowen had taken the lead at the Grove and it was another own goal, this time from Mark Freeman. The big defender inadvertently deflected a shot with his head past Robins 'keeper Kevin Maloy to give the Yeltz a fortunate advantage. The scoreline remained the same until the hour mark, when something special began to happen that would transform Cheltenham's season. Knight, playing against the club he had recently left to rejoin Cheltenham, lashed an unstoppable drive into the top corner of Mark Hart's near post to level the scores. It was the winger's second goal against his former club in as many games and Halesowen must have been wishing that they had never let him leave.

Cheltenham began to take complete control against a shell-shocked Yeltz side and loan-signing from Barnet Richard Dunwell scored two in quick succession. The speedy forward's first was a stunning strike that flew past Hart's outstretched arms and into the roof of the net. He then drilled home a penalty after he had been tripped in the area after another powerful run. With the game now beyond them, Halesowen capitulated and Darren Wright added another to his impressive scoring run in the latter half of the season. Wright's fine strike was followed by another good goal from Martin Boyle, who claimed his thirteenth of the season.

Everything Cheltenham hit seemed to fly into the net and Boyle's goal completed a remarkable comeback for Cotterill's buoyant troops. None of it was heralded in the first sixty minutes. It looked as though the script was going to be all too familiar when a power header by Jamie Victory from a corner hit the underside of the bar and stayed out in the eleventh minute.

Maloy beat away an angled blast by Evran Wright, the premier division's leading scorer with twenty-six, but when Freeman, facing goal, slid in before Maloy and turned in John Snape's teasing low centre, the alarm bells rang loud and clear. There was a moment right on half-time which Maloy would prefer to forget. Kevin Harrison tried to lob him from forty yards and Maloy at first made no move. He eventually realised he would have to but when he went for it he missed it and the ball hit a post and bounced against his back. The way things had been going at that time it should have gone in, but it stayed out and everything turned out dramatically different after Knight's shining strike.

There was one save for Maloy, from Gary Hackett when it was 1–1, but once Dunwell had made his spectacular contribution, it became more and more embarrassing for Halesowen. Striker Jason Eaton went on for the last three minutes, his first appearance in the Dr Marten's League since he was forced to rest a back injury on 14 December. This superb result put Cheltenham in the perfect frame of mind for the visit of the Tigers two days later. The large Cheltenham presence at the Grove stayed behind long after the final whistle singing and rightly celebrating a fantastic away performance.

Caretaker manager Steve Cotterill said he felt very sorry for Halesowen's manager Stewart Hall, whom he saw looking shell-shocked in the car park after the game. Cotterill also paid tribute to the

Darren Wright scored number four against shell-shocked Halesowen Town.

travelling supporters, as well as the home fans, who applauded his side off the field and again when they walked into the clubhouse afterwards. This was only Cotterill's thirteenth match in charge, but the massive impact he was having on his newly inherited team was already beginning to show. Cheltenham went on to lose only one of their last seven fixtures, snatching runners-up spot behind champions Gresley Rovers to earn a return to the Conference after a five-season absence. Halesowen, who were runners-up to Rushden & Diamonds the previous season, ended up in fourth, one point behind Cheltenham and below third-placed Gloucester on goal difference.

Halesowen Town: Hart, Clarke, Bradley, Owen, Snape, Evans, Harrison (Bellingham 76), Wright, Halsall, Shearer, Hackett (Sharpe 76). Subs not used: Gardiner.
Cheltenham Town: Maloy, Chenoweth (Eaton 84), Knight, Banks, Freeman, Victory, Howells, Wright, Dunwell, Boyle, Bloomer. Subs not used: Duff, Cotterill
Referee: F.G. Stretton (Nottingham).
Attendance: 1,406.

MATCH 21: BURTON ALBION V. CHELTENHAM TOWN

Dr Marten's League Premier Division
Saturday 3 May 1997, Eton Park
Burton Albion 0 Cheltenham Town 0

The climax to the 1996/97 season could not have been any more tense as the promotion race between bitter local rivals Cheltenham Town and Gloucester City boiled down to the final day. The Robins held a slight advantage over the Tigers and as they travelled to Burton Albion's Eton Park, knew that they had to equal or better City's result against Salisbury City to claim a place in the Conference after a five-year absence.

Cheltenham had become the nearly men of the Southern League, having finished as runners-up to Dover Athletic, Farnborough Town and Hednesford Town in 1993, 1994 and 1995 respectively, as well as a third-place finish in 1996. On this occasion they knew that second place would be good enough to secure their return to the top flight of non-league football due to runaway champions Gresley Rovers' ground not meeting the required standards for promotion.

A large Cheltenham presence in the crowd, many armed with radios to keep up with events at Meadow Park, gave their heroes a rapturous tickertape welcome and prepared themselves for the afternoon of drama that was about to unfold. Burton were a difficult proposition, particularly on their own pitch, and they had already won the Dr Marten's Cup and the Birmingham Senior Cup, which they paraded to their supporters at half-time.

Manager John Barton's Brewers were without forceful midfielder Darren Stride, who was suspended. Chances in the first half were few and far between and a Jamie Victory effort in the tenth minute proved to be the only notable stop Albion goalkeeper Darren Acton had to make. There were suddenly hundreds of worried faces as news began the filter around the ground that Gloucester had taken the lead through an own goal from former Robin Matt Lovell in the twentieth minute. Lovell inadvertently turned in a cross from another ex-Cheltenham player, Chris Burns. City had progressed to the semi-finals of the FA Trophy, where they lost out to Dagenham and Redbridge, but their run resulted in a fixture pile-up which hampered their chances of pipping Cheltenham to a place in the Conference.

Defender Chris Banks saved Cheltenham after thirty-four minutes when a clearing punch from Kevin Maloy went straight to Steve Spooner, who floated it back over Maloy for Banks to head away before it dropped in. Banks was booked for tugging former Cheltenham striker Micky Nuttell's shirt – the pair had been sent off for an altercation in the 3–3 draw between the two clubs at Whaddon Road less than two months earlier. Shortly before half-time, Burton lost Charlie Palmer, a central defender who had played over 500 games in the Football League. Bob Bloomer, who had broken his nose during a 0–0 home draw with Newport seven days earlier, clipped the top of the crossbar with a free-kick, but at the interval, manager Leroy Rosenior's Gloucester were on course to steal the promotion berth from their arch-enemies. However, there were still forty-five dramatic minutes left to be played.

As Burton continued to keep Cheltenham out, Salisbury equalised at Gloucester through Lee Webb and the complexion of the afternoon changed further when the Robins were awarded a sixty-sixth-minute penalty after Lee Howells was tripped. However, loan signing from Barnet Richard Dunwell saw his spot kick saved well by Acton and the tension continued to mount. Brave Burton were reduced to ten men after seventy minutes due to an injury sustained by Spooner when all three of their substitutes had been used. Still Cheltenham could not break Burton down, but news that Gloucester's David Johnson had been sent off for the second match in succession for a professional foul, and a second goal for Salisbury from Robbie Harbut, eased the pressure. There was then a roar around the ground and fans in the stand jumped out of their seats as word spread that Salisbury had

Richard Dunwell misses from the penalty spot.

scored a third through Harbut's second against an exhausted Tigers side, for whom a run of seven games in fifteen days proved to be too much. Just before the end, there were reports of a pitch invasion delaying the match at Gloucester as the occasion got the better of some of the Tigers followers, one of whom attacked referee Ian Whelan.

Victory, scorer of nine goals from left-back during his first season in non-league football, headed over the bar before former Burton player Cotterill went onto the pitch he knew so well in the eighty-eighth minute, but it remained goalless. The final whistle blew and after confirmation that the Gloucester game had restarted and finished 3–1 in Salisbury's favour, the celebrations began in earnest as most of the 500 travelling fans poured onto the pitch. Welsh international goalkeeper Martin Thomas, who had left Cheltenham the previous season to concentrate on his successful coaching career, was among the delighted spectators.

A promotion race that went to the bitter end – but ended in glory – triggered the start of a wonderful few years for Cheltenham. Cotterill, caretaker player-manager until promotion was secured, was offered a full-time contract with the club and the Robins climbed to the heights of Division Two (now League One) within five years. The Bournemouth-based thirty-two-year-old was unable to continue playing in the Conference due to an insurance payment he took when knee injuries put him out of the full-time game.

Cheltenham took on Gloucester in the final of the Gloucestershire Senior Cup just three days after their day of destiny in the league, with the Robins winning 2–1 at Meadow Park to compound the misery for the Tigers. Cheltenham chairman Arthur Hayward stepped down at the end of the season, opening the way for Paul Baker to take over and oversee the club's elevation to the Football League two years later.

The celebrations could finally begin after five years of frustration.

Burton Albion: Acton, Davies, Titterton, Keast, Palmer (Benton 44), Spooner, Lyons (Marlowe 70), Redfern, Nuttell, Devaney (Ejiofor 70), Hornby.
Cheltenham Town: Maloy, Duff, Knight, Banks, Freeman, Victory, Howells, Wright, Dunwell (Boyle 80), Eaton (Cotterill 89), Bloomer.
Referee: M. Dexter (Leicester).
Attendance: 1,142.

Match 22: Cheltenham Town v. Halifax Town

GM Vauxhall Conference
Saturday 1 November 1998, Whaddon Road
Cheltenham Town 4 (Eaton 61, 62, 72,
 Bloomer 67)
Halifax Town 0

Cheltenham Town sent a message out to the whole of non-league football by stunning previously unbeaten GM Vauxhall Conference leaders Halifax Town 4–0 at Whaddon Road. Former Football League club Halifax had been revived by sixty-year-old manager George Mulhall, who was the oldest manager in the Conference. He had taken over at The Shay near the end of the previous season when Halifax were in real danger of being relegated from the Conference, a mere three years after dropping out of the League. Mulhall's side were unbeaten twelve matches into the season, but that run was ended rather abruptly as Cheltenham scored four goals during a magical twelve-minute spell in front of a healthy crowd.

The two leading scorers in the Conference came up against each other and Halifax's Geoff Horsfield, who was soon to progress to play at the highest level, was well and truly eclipsed by Cheltenham's Jason Eaton. The match was played on the day of Horsfield's twenty-fourth birthday. The Barnsley-born striker went on to train with Cheltenham, on trial, during the summer of 2008.

Eaton claimed a hat-trick and Bob Bloomer scored one of the most spectacular Cheltenham goals for years as Steve Cotterill's side continued to make an astonishing impact following their promotion from the Southern League. Bloomer's strike reflected the way things had been going for Cheltenham after they returned to the upper echelon of the non-league game. His volley flew past goalkeeper Lee Martin after Dale Watkins, way out on the left, had brought down on his toe a long overhead hoist by Lee Howells, and laid it back straight away to Jimmy Smith. Smith, on the left of the midfield, immediately scooped a first-time pass towards the box and Bloomer's left foot met it two feet from the ground, twenty yards out. That goal was the third and was scored in the sixty-eighth minute, five minutes after Halifax had been knocked groggy by two goals in two minutes from Eaton. He jumped inside Martin for a corner taken by Keith Knight on the left and the ball went in ultra-slowly off the left post.

It took a few moments for it to sink in that a goal had been scored but the second was very visible. Central defender Brian Kilcline, thirty-six and in his third match for Halifax after a long and illustrious career at the top, slipped and missed a cross. Eaton was left all on his own and his shot, possibly mis-hit, screwed over Martin and from nowhere Cheltenham were suddenly leading 2–0. Bloomer's blast was followed by another from Eaton in the seventy-fourth minute. It stemmed from a free-kick which was cleared back as far as taker, Knight. Knight's return into the box produced a scramble which ended with Eaton scoring his twelfth league goal to go level in the scoring chart with Halifax's Geoff Horsfield. The four-goal spell took the breath away because it was in stark contrast to a tight and virtually chance-free first half. Martin made one save from a shot by Watkins when he was moving in from the left, but that was about the sum of the shots-on-goal scene.

Before the rush of goals in the second half, Dale Watkins had given two signs that Halifax's defence, which had given away only seven goals in twelve games, was not impenetrable. He forced full-back Mark Bradshaw to clear a header from the line after Jamie Victory's head had flicked on a corner and Kieran O'Regan covered back to kick away an angled shot after Watkins had gone round Martin. Halifax, dazed by events, spent the last fifteen minutes trying to repair the damage and even Jimmy Smith was back to make a vital headed clearance when a cross from the left was about to drop on the head of substitute Darren Lyons.

Jason Eaton was a thorn in Halifax's side.

Cheltenham, possibly a little over-affected early on by Halifax's record that season, took some time to start moving smoothly in the first half. Midfielders Ian Brown and Jamie Paterson threatened to dictate the game but a heavy tackle on Howells left Brown limping and Halifax's initial chest-beating soon died down. Howells was booked midway through the half for a late tackle on Gary Brook and Halifax's Chris Hurst was cautioned in the last minute of the half after jumping two-footed at Chris Banks.

Half-time turned out to be a watershed. Three of the goals may not have been masterpieces but they had not been predictable. In the end, the result will have made the other clubs in the Conference take note. Eaton was given a standing ovation when he was replaced by Darren Wright five minutes from the end. Watkins and Smith were both substituted in the last two minutes.

After his stunning goal, Bloomer, thirty-one at the time, said, 'It was my left foot as well. Sometimes a chance falls to you and you get a good strike on it. It worked a treat. I won't be setting any goal targets. I will just keep seeing them hit the back of the net and count them at the end of the season!'

Halifax recovered from their Whaddon Road set-back to take the Conference title and return to the Football League. Cheltenham faced a major fixture backlog due to their FA Cup and FA Trophy runs, but went on to finish second, their highest ever finish. The two teams drew 1–1 at The Shay the day Halifax were presented with the Conference trophy in front of more than 6,000 supporters.

Cheltenham Town: Book, Duff, Victory, Banks, Freeman, Smith (Benton 89), Howells, Knight, Eaton (Wright 85), Watkins (Crisp 88), Bloomer.
Halifax Town: Martin, Thackeray, Bradshaw, O'Regan, Kilcline, Stoneman, Paterson, Hurst (Lyons 65), Brook, Horsfield, Brown. Subs not used: Griffiths, Horner. Subs not used: Griffiths, Horner.
Referee: G.A. Beale (Taunton).
Attendance: 2,508.

Match 23: Cheltenham Town v. Reading

FA Cup Third Round
Tuesday 13 January 1998, Whaddon Road
Cheltenham Town 1 (Watkins 23 pen)
Reading 1 (Morley 71)

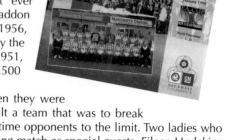

The biggest crowd at Whaddon Road since 1956/57 gathered to see Cheltenham, then in the Conference, take on Championship strugglers Reading in the FA Cup Third Round. With previous wins over Thatcham Town, Merthyr Tydfil, Paulton Rovers, Sutton United, Tiverton Town and Boreham Wood, Steve Cotterill's Robins had already equalled their best ever performance in the Cup. Cheltenham's record Whaddon Road attendance had been set against Reading in 1956, when they met for a first-round tie that was won 2–1 by the visitors. The two clubs also met in the first round in 1951, when Reading won 3–1 at Elm Park in front of 16,500 supporters.

Cheltenham reached the third round in 1934, when they were beaten 3–1 by Blackpool, but Steve Cotterill had built a team that was to break numerous club records and his side pushed their full-time opponents to the limit. Two ladies who watched the Robins play Blackpool attended the Reading match as special guests. Eileen Hodgkins and Hilda Read were both in attendance, with Hilda wearing the same rosette she wore in 1934!

The tie was originally scheduled to be played on Saturday 3 January, but heavy overnight rain waterlogged the Whaddon Road pitch and Cheltenham's first taste of third-round action for sixty-four years was delayed for ten days. Referee Ken Leach had no choice but to call the eagerly anticipated game off at 9.30 a.m. The postponement meant that Reading were without Carl Asaba, an £800,000 club record signing from Brentford two days before the start of the season, who started a three-match suspension. However, the reschedule allowed Royals' ball-winning midfielder Phil Parkinson to play after recovering from a pelvic injury. For Cheltenham, main goal hope Dale Watkins was battling on with a thigh strain sustained in the second round replay at Boreham Wood, as well as a hamstring pull picked up at Yeovil on New Year's Day, when a seventeen-match unbeaten run had come to an end.

Reading were struggling at the foot of their division and were clearly lacking in confidence. This was in stark contrast to a buoyant Robins side who looked capable of giving anyone a game. After raiding upfield straight from kick-off, Cheltenham were forced to back-pedal while Reading forced five corners in the first ten minutes. Full-back Steve Swales forced goalkeeper Steve Book to drop at a post for the first serious save as wingers Jason Bowen and James Lambert made a bright start for the Royals. Parkinson's shot hit Chris Banks and Lee Hodges fired at Book before Cheltenham began to show they were not there to be walked all over.

Manager Steve Cotterill's Robins were awarded a penalty after twenty-three minutes for a foul on Clive Walker by Gareth Davies, who later admitted the veteran was one of the hardest players he had to mark all season. Summer signing from Gloucester City Watkins shut out the pain and scored emphatically from the spot to leave the home fans looking on in disbelief. It was difficult to tell which set of players were the professionals as the home side dictated long periods of the game. Within minutes of the penalty, a long-range header by Bob Bloomer dropped over the bar with goalkeeper Nicky Hammond scampering and Hammond's quick fall stopped a diving header by Victory on the line as Reading lost some of their composure.

Keith Knight shot high and close when Victory flicked on and Watkins lifted an angled lob over the bar as half-time was welcomed more by Reading than Cheltenham. Book made one of the finest saves of his season when he appeared from nowhere at the foot of his right post to cut out a ground shot through milling players by Davies in the fifty-eighth minute. Five minutes later, Watkins was deemed to be onside when Bloomer's pass reached him in front of goal, but his shot on the turn slammed into Hammond and another good Cheltenham chance had gone. Jimmy Smith, who had worked exceptionally hard on the left of midfield, was replaced by Steve Benton after seventy minutes, but he had barely stepped onto the pitch when Trevor Morley brought some relief to Reading. Cheltenham had held on to their lead for fifty minutes, more than matching the Royals, but the surface was still sodden on a wet night and former West Ham striker Morley's low shot squirmed agonisingly under the body of Book in the mud to keep Reading in the tie.

Former Reading player Knight had a late chance to win the game for Cheltenham when Andy Bernal allowed Bloomer's pass to reach him, but his powerful shot screamed inches over and Cheltenham would have to visit Elm Park for a replay. With a fourth-round trip to Cardiff City at stake, Cheltenham travelled to Reading and once again gave a tremendous effort against a side three levels above them in the pyramid. Morley was on target for the Royals again in the thirty-eighth minute of the replay, but cup veteran Clive Walker scored an equaliser six minutes after half-time as Cheltenham gave another exceptional account of themselves. Walker darted in at the far post after Jason Eaton had headed back Watkins' cross from the left. Martyn Booty broke Cheltenham hearts in the seventy-second minute with a long-range winner. Seven minutes from the end Jamie Victory's shot was going wide, but it hit Watkins and was diverted at speed against the inside of the near post as Cheltenham came within a whisker of taking the tie to extra-time.

Dale Watkins lifts the roof at Whaddon Road after scoring his first-half penalty.

Almost 10,000 people stood and saluted Cotterill's braves, with the home fans applauding the non-leaguers, even chanting Chelt-en-ham in the way they had heard it from 2,000 proud throats. Cotterill told his devastated players to hold their heads high after the game and assured them that they would be going to Wembley in the FA Trophy in May, which of course, they did. Relieved Royals boss Terry Bullivant hailed the efforts of Cheltenham after the replay, stating that Cotterill's side were good enough to make it into the Football League and they fulfilled Bullivant's claims the following season by winning the Conference title.

Cheltenham Town: Book, Duff, Victory, Banks, Freeman, Knight, Howells, Walker (Eaton 75), Smith (Benton 70), Watkins, Bloomer. Subs not used: Crisp, Wright, Milton.
Reading: Hammond, Booty, Swales, Bernal, Davies, Parkinson, Bowen, Hodges (Caskey 84), Morley, Lovell (Meaker 80). Subs not used: Thorp, Bibbo, Glasgow.
Referee: K.A. Leach (Staffs).
Attendance: 6,000.

MATCH 24: DOVER ATHLETIC V. CHELTENHAM TOWN

FA Trophy Semi-Final second leg
Saturday 4 April 1998, Crabble Athletic Ground
Dover Athletic 2 (Le Bihan 70, Budden 78)
Cheltenham Town 2 (Watkins 6, Eaton 33)

Cheltenham Town made the long cross-country journey to Kent, knowing that a draw would be good enough to take them to Wembley after a thrilling 2–1 win at Whaddon Road in the first leg of their semi-final against Dover Athletic. Jason Eaton had scored twice as the Robins came from behind to overcome Gerald Dobbs' early opener for Dover. Dover had greeted Cheltenham's return to the Vauxhall Conference, after a five-season absence, by beating them 3–0 at Crabble on the opening day.

The clubs had played each other in the Trophy twice before and Dover had won both times. The first was in the opening round on 2 December 1972 when Bill Bailey scored Cheltenham's goal in a 2–1 defeat at Whaddon Road. The other was in 1995 when the Lilywhites won 1–0 in a first-round second replay after a 2–2 draw at Dover (Darren Wright two) and a 1–1 draw in Cheltenham (Chris Banks).

It was a special day for Robins midfielder Russell Milton, who left Dover to join Cheltenham the previous summer after relocating to the area from Kent. Dover reached the semi-finals on penalties against Barrow and their manager, Bill Williams, warned before the game that his side would batter Cheltenham physically. The Cheltenham players stayed up later than their manager wanted them to the night before the game, watching the video of the first leg. However, already one goal to the good, Cheltenham made a dream start to the second leg when Dale Watkins, who had been outstanding all season, put his side ahead after six minutes with a spectacular scissors kick for his twenty-fourth of the season. Watkins had endured the sour taste of semi-final defeat twice in the previous three years and this time he was determined to savour Wembley. He cried after Rushden & Diamonds lost 2–1 to a Woking side including Clive Walker, after leading in the first leg in 1995. Rushden, then in the Southern League, felt they were unlucky to lose. The Peterborough-based forward was angry when Gloucester City lost 2–1 to Dagenham and Redbridge in a replay in 1997 after the first two legs had ended in a 2–2 draw after extra-time.

There was a carnival atmosphere in the away end as Robins fans envisaged their heroes walking out of the tunnel and playing in the shadows of the famous twin towers for the first time. Things were to get even better for Steve Cotterill's men before half-time as Eaton picked the perfect moment to net his 100th goal for Cheltenham and make it 2–0. Eaton's thirty-third minute strike had a touch of good fortune about it as a clearance hit him and flew into the net, but it appeared to be the goal that would ensure a place against Southport in the final as Cheltenham led 4–1 on aggregate.

However, the second half was a different story and Dover showed great fighting spirit to claw their way back into the tie. They produced two goals in quick succession; both of the highest quality, and suddenly Cheltenham found themselves up against it. First Neil Le Bihan unleashed a stunning left-foot shot that curled around the outstretched arms of 'keeper Steve Book. Eight minutes later, John Budden scored another spectacular goal and suddenly there were some worried faces among the travelling contingent.

Cheltenham managed to stop the Lilywhites' mini goal-of-the-season competition and no further goals followed. Paul Durkin blew the whistle to end the tension and the Robins had made history. Cotterill and his men showed the utmost respect for their defeated opponents after the game, shaking hands and walking off the pitch in a sensible manner. Cotterill did not want his side whooping in the tunnel and rubbing it in devastated Dover's faces. After a short spell in the changing rooms, Cotterill

Jason Eaton joins in with the jubilant celebrations at Dover.

and his team re-emerged to scenes of jubilation and the reality began to set in that after 106 years of underachievement, Cheltenham would be playing in their first major final.

Paul Futcher's Southport overcame Slough 2–1 on aggregate in the other last-four tie, setting up a May date with Cheltenham at Wembley, where thirty-three-year-old Cotterill would become the youngest manager to lead a team out for a Trophy final. Cotterill was the one more than 700 chanting, exultant fans called for when they had finished congratulating the players. He quickly dedicated the win to the club's loyal fans and to long-serving physio Wally Attwood, who had passed away earlier in the season.

The last club Cheltenham played before the Trophy final was Southport, in the Vauxhall Conference, fifteen days before their showdown. And the first club they played after the semi-final success was Dover, in the Conference, three days after ending their Wembley dream. Chairman Paul Baker, Cotterill, secretary Reg Woodward and director Brian Sandland went to a meeting at Wembley three days after the semi-final win to find out what they had to do before the final.

Dover Athletic: Mitten (Davies 46), Munday, Palmer, Budden, Shearer, Stebbing, Dobbs (Jones 68), Strouts, Ayorinde, Le Bihan, Henry.

Cheltenham Town: Book, Duff, Banks, Freeman, Victory, Milton (Wright 74), Howells, Walker, Eaton, Watkins, Bloomer.

Referee: P. Durkin (Portland).

Attendance: 3,240.

Match 25: Cheltenham Town v. Southport

FA Umbro Trophy Final
Sunday 17 May 1998, Wembley Stadium
Cheltenham Town 1 (Eaton 79) Southport 0

The town of Cheltenham was gripped by football fever like never before as the Robins reached their first major final in 1998. Victories over Enfield, Rushden & Diamonds, Ashton United, Hayes and Dover Athletic took Steve Cotterill's Cheltenham side to Wembley Stadium for the climax of what was already the finest season in the club's history. The build-up to the big occasion created a buzz around the town with tickets selling like hotcakes and interest spreading across the whole of Gloucestershire. The squad even recorded a cup final record 'Cotswold Pride' at Cheltenham's Planet Rock studios, but with lyrics such as, 'Bob won't drop Bloomers, according to rumours,' the top of the charts was never a possibility!

Cotterill, the home-grown hero who had masterminded Cheltenham's remarkable transformation, was only thirty-three years and ten months old, making him the youngest manager ever to lead a side out at the home of football in a major cup final. Before the game, national interest focused on Cheltenham's Clive Walker, who was playing in his fourth final in five years, a month before his forty-first birthday. It was his sixth Wembley appearance in total, but he never managed a goal beneath the Twin Towers. He was also stuck one goal short of a century of non-league goals going into the final. He failed to break his Wembley duck, but his reputation as a lucky charm in the non-league version of the FA Cup was enhanced.

Southport's player-manager Paul Futcher was forty-one years and 234 days, making him the oldest man on the pitch. The match was refereed by Gary Willard, who had walked off the pitch for four minutes in the Premiership match between Barnsley and Liverpool at Oakwell earlier that season.

The teams were presented to guest of honour, World Cup hero Roger Hunt, just twenty-four hours after the FA Cup final when Arsenal defeated Newcastle United 2–0. Hunt had earlier presented all five of Cheltenham non-league international stars with their England caps. Chris Banks, Dale Watkins, Jamie Victory, Neil Grayson and Lee Howells all appeared for England in a 2–1 win over Holland at Crawley.

After all the hype, the day of the game finally arrived and in true cup final tradition, it was gloriously sunny weather. The match itself was by no means a classic, but it was nonetheless a memorable day for the 18,000 or so Robins fans who made the trip to London, leaving Cheltenham like a ghost town.

Southport overcame Slough Town in the semi-finals, 2–1 on aggregate. The Sandgrounders finished sixteenth in the Conference and twenty-eight points behind runners-up Cheltenham and began the final as firm underdogs. Big match nerves appeared to have affected some of the players and there were uncharacteristic mistakes aplenty.

However, Bob Bloomer made a fantastic last-ditch challenge to deny Sandgrounders' skipper Brian Butler a goalscoring chance, and Steve Book's handling was impeccable as Futcher's men controlled large periods of the game. Brian Ross wasted a chance for Southport in the sixty-third minute, when he evaded the challenge of Mark Freeman and was faced with only Book to beat. Book did well to make himself big, giving Ross very little of the goal to aim for and the chance was gone. Book capped a fine first season with an outstanding display on the big stage. The previous time he was with a club who played there, he had not been involved; he had just joined Wycombe Wanderers after spending most of the 1993/94 season with Brighton. Wycombe reached the play-off final in their first season as a Football League club, but Book was left out, so he went for a game of

Main man Jason Eaton heads the winner (left) and poses with the trophy (right).

cricket and listened to the game on the radio. Book's father, Kim, conceded eight goals to Manchester United in the FA Cup thirty years earlier, George Best scoring six of them, but Book Junior surpassed himself to shut Southport out.

The Sandgrounders created the best chances, but they lacked composure in front of goal and as the game wore on, Cheltenham looked more and more threatening. With eleven minutes to go, Cheltenham made the breakthrough and two substitutes were involved in the lead up to the goal. First Jimmy Smith, who had replaced Keith Knight, teased Ged Kielty on the right wing and after some fancy footwork, the diminutive Scot was fouled by the Southport defender. Russell Milton, on in place of Walker, floated in one of his trademark free-kicks, which was flicked on by Jamie Victory for Jason Eaton to head the ball past Billy Stewart and into the back of the net to send the Robins fans wild.

Despite not performing to the best of their ability, Cheltenham showed fighting spirit and determination to emerge victorious, leaving the whole town on a high. Banks climbed the thirty-nine steps to collect the FA Trophy and the unprecedented celebrations began. The open-top bus tour the following day will live on long in the memories of all who witnessed their heroes celebrating the first major piece of silverware in the history of the club. Cheltenham turned out in force to cheer its heroes, who made their way through the town centre, and the interest and money generated from the Trophy success laid the foundations for the club's promotion to the Football League a year later. Cheltenham had been replaced in the Conference by Woking in 1992, but they succeeded the same club as Trophy holders six years later, Cheltenham almost reached Wembley the following season in their final FA Trophy campaign to date, but they lost out to eventual winners Kingstonian in the semi-finals.

Cheltenham Town: Book, Duff, Victory, Banks, Freeman, Knight (Smith 78), Howells, Bloomer, Eaton, Watkins, Walker (Milton 78). Sub not used: Wright.
Southport: Stewart, Horner, Futcher, Ryan, Farley, Kielty, Butler, Gamble, Formby (Whittaker 80), Thompson (Bolland 86), Ross. Sub not used: Mitten.
Referee: G. Willard (Worthing)
Attendance: 26, 837

Match 26: Rushden & Diamonds v. Cheltenham Town

Nationwide Conference
Saturday 3 April 1999, Nene Park
Rushden & Diamonds 1 (de Souza 21)
Cheltenham Town 2 (Freeman 90, Grayson 90)

Cheltenham Town's trip to Nationwide Conference title rivals Rushden & Diamonds turned out to be one of the most memorable games in the history of the club, and arguably the most important of all. This was not the day that Cheltenham secured the championship, but it will be forever remembered as the day when the tide turned in their favour and Football League destiny was firmly within their own grasp. It was the manner of the victory that made that Easter Saturday afternoon so special and it is usually referred to as 'The Rushden Comeback'.

Boss Steve Cotterill's men went into the match sitting third in the table, one point behind Rushden, with a game in hand. The game created a huge amount of interest and more fans made the trip to Northamptonshire than Rushden could have dreamed of. Many disappointed fans were locked outside the stadium – the only sad sight on an otherwise wonderful day – one of the highest crowds ever assembled for a Conference fixture gathered in anticipation.

Rushden's Michael McElhatton had the first goal attempt with a firm shot which went wide and Robins striker Dennis Bailey watched a long attempt at a chip drop over the bar after five minutes. Darren Collins, Rushden's leading scorer with fifteen in the Conference, headed wide and right-back Tim Wooding's well-hit shot from twenty yards went past a post as Rushden made a positive start. They took the lead after twenty-one minutes through Miquel de Souza, who made one FA Cup appearance for Cheltenham against Birmingham City in the first-round tie of 1990. The goal was the outcome of a free-kick given away by a head-high challenge on Paul Underwood by Michael Duff, who was booked for his misdemeanour. Midfielder Guy Branston nodded down Darren Bradshaw's free-kick and de Souza was free to prod the ball past Steve Book from close range.

Rushden had edged the opening half an hour, but from that moment onwards Cheltenham were always on top, not giving Rushden another chance, but an equaliser proved elusive. Duff struck a shot against the post and David Norton forced a fine save from Mark Smith in the Rushden goal. From the corner, shots by Norton and Neil Howarth were blocked. Soon, another Norton shot was being tipped away and suddenly Cheltenham, calm and collected, were in control. Robins skipper Chris Banks swept with elegance, having missed the previous two visits to Nene Park which had both ended in 4–1 defeats. Banks had made his Cheltenham debut on the same ground in a 2–0 win in 1994 and de Souza's goal aside, his five-man back line looked relatively comfortable.

Mark Freeman, who had been sent off amid ugly scenes in the corresponding fixture a year earlier, replaced Neil Howarth after sixty-three minutes and Russell Milton went on in place of Bob Bloomer. Ex-QPR striker Bailey's interest in the game ended when he sustained a leg injury in the sixty-eighth minute. He limped on for five minutes before Keith Knight, who had also been sent off at Rushden the previous season, replaced him. But it was big 'Boka' Freeman who was soon to banish the painful memories of previous clashes with Diamonds. As time began to run out, a corner was taken quickly, initially against the wishes of Cotterill who barked from the dugout that he wanted a delay to allow players to push forward into the penalty area, but Duff swung in a cross from the left. It was not a high, dropping cross, rather a head-high one which curled beyond everyone until it reached Freeman, who stooped to head in at the far post to send the Cheltenham supporters delirious. It was right in front of the red and white bank of fans and they erupted. Freeman ran across to them, arms aloft to milk the applause.

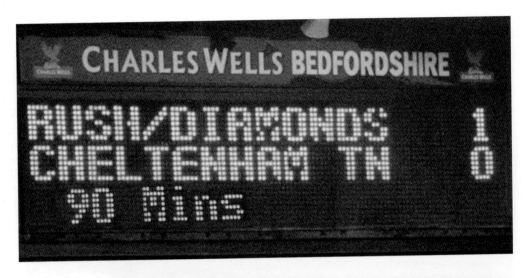

*The rapidly
changing
scoreboard at
Nene Park.*

With ninety minutes already showing on the prominent electronic scoreboard at Nene Park, Cheltenham would have settled for a point, but with the fans still celebrating Freeman's leveller, the improbable happened. Freeman was involved again, hoisting the ball high over the Rushden defence and it fell to Brough who had been pushed up front where he had developed a habit of causing mayhem. Brough tried to lob the ball over the advancing Smith, but he miscued his effort and brushed it across the goal line, where Grayson lunged towards the ball with defender Jim Rodwell. The ball hit the back of the net from Grayson's left foot and in a matter of seconds the whole complexion of the Conference title race had been transformed.

The post-match celebrations showed just how much it meant to Cheltenham and their travelling hordes of more than 2,000. Injured players such as Jason Eaton and Richard Walker who were both in plaster, the hobbling Mark Yates and the recovering Dale Watkins rushed over to join in the party in front of the impressive Air Wair Stand. For Freeman, who said at the time he would be happy to just play one game in the Football League, it was a high moment of his career. Released by Wolverhampton Wanderers as a youngster, he had more disappointment when Hednesford Town let him go after he had helped them win promotion to the Conference in 1995, but while at Cheltenham he finally fulfilled his dream, playing sixty-five Football League games for the Robins between 1999 and 2001 before departing for Boston United in a £15,000 deal.

Neil Grayson (left) and Jamie Victory (right) congratulate Mark Freeman on his leveller.

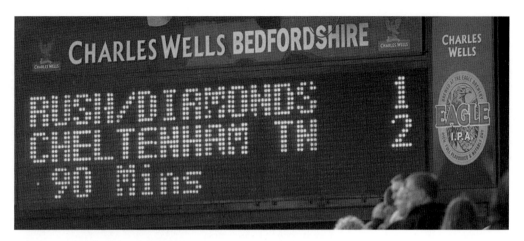

The final score that changed the complexion of the Conference title race.

Rushden were shell-shocked and Brian Talbot's demoralised side's challenge fell away badly. They dropped two more points on Easter Monday, drawing 1–1 with Woking and finally ended up in fourth place. Cheltenham followed up this huge victory with another crucial win over Kidderminster Harriers, eventually sealing the crown nineteen days later with an equally thrilling 3–2 home win over Yeovil Town. Rushden had to wait two more years to finally win promotion from the Conference.

Rushden & Diamonds: Smith, Wooding, Bradshaw, Rodwell, Underwood, McElhatton, Branston, Cooper, Heggs, de Souza, Collins.
Cheltenham Town: Book, Duff, Banks, Brough, Howarth (Freeman 63), Victory, Howells, Bloomer (Milton 63), Norton, Grayson, Bailey (Knight 73).
Referee: Mr S. French (Wolverhampton).
Attendance: 6,312

MATCH 27: CHELTENHAM TOWN V. YEOVIL TOWN

Nationwide Conference
Thursday 22 April 1999, Whaddon Road
Cheltenham Town 3 (Victory 4, Grayson 22, Duff 90)
Yeovil Town 2 (Pickard 2, Patmore 47 pen)

Cheltenham Town clinched promotion to the Football League in the most dramatic of circumstances on what is probably still the greatest of all nights in the club's history. Nine months of hard work came to fruition for the Robins as they sealed the Nationwide Conference title on their own turf with three games to spare after a truly epic encounter against Yeovil Town. Cheltenham went into the Thursday night game knowing that a win would seal the championship, but what unfolded was one of the most extraordinary matches ever witnessed at Whaddon Road. After a kick off delayed by fifteen minutes due to the huge volume of fans, Yeovil, who had an outside chance of taking the title themselves, were determined to spoil the party and took the lead after eighty-two seconds. Their scorer was Owen Pickard, who had been a transfer target for Cheltenham boss Steve Cotterill in 1997.

Jamie Victory settled Cheltenham nerves, forcing home an equaliser from close range at the third attempt after a goalmouth scramble. Neil Grayson then put Cheltenham within touching distance of the League after twenty-two minutes, powering home a near-post header from a Michael Duff cross for his sixteenth Conference goal of the season. There was an electric atmosphere inside the ground and Yeovil hit back soon after half-time to change the mood in the crowd once again. Victory handled a cross inside the area and Warren Patmore made no mistake from the spot. With the scores level, Paul Steele was sent off for Yeovil and Cheltenham went in search of a winner. They bombarded Tony Pennock's goal with shots flying in from all angles. Pennock was in inspired form and seemed to be unbeatable, making saves from Grayson, John Brough and David Norton. The breathtaking display of goalkeeping may have meant that Cheltenham would have to put champagne on ice, but the deadlock was finally broken seven minutes into injury time. Keith Knight floated in a free-kick from the right, Duff and Victory rose in unison and the ball was headed past a stranded Pennock to send Whaddon Road into raptures. Who had scored the goal was unclear at the time and although it was officially credited to Duff, Victory still maintains that he made contact. Victory said, 'To score the winning goal was great. I came across and Duffo came behind me but I got the touch for the goal.'

It did not really matter as Cheltenham had achieved something special and there were tears of joy from Cotterill and jubilant scenes from players and fans alike as the reality set in that Cheltenham would have a full-time club for the first time. One of the most ecstatic players at the final whistle was midfielder David Norton who had laid a ghost, achieving his burning desire to win promotion for Cheltenham Town. He was captain of Hereford United when they lost their Football League place in 1997, a day he described as the worst of his football life. After the Yeovil game, Norton said:

What happened that day was something I will never forget. I looked at the clippings this morning, but that's gone now, finished with. It was incredible tonight. You go behind, get back, go ahead, get pulled back again and miss about four chances . . . and then we've done it. My sole objective this season was to win the league and get my pride back. Cheltenham and Steve Cotterill gave me another chance when I didn't even know whether I could kick a ball. Right from the off we said we could win it and now we have. I've given everything to this club because they have given everything to me. I had seventeen years in the pro game, I played for England Youth and at Anfield and Old Trafford, but nothing in the world can compare with this tonight.

Michael Duff and Jamie Victory jump in unison to head Cheltenham into the Football League.

Cotterill, who had transformed his hometown club beyond recognition, said:

It's down to the players and the whole spirit within the town. I've done nothing but tell them all season that they could win the league. I told them from the first day of pre-season training in July. It's fantastic. I know I'm biased and bound to say this, but they have got what they deserve. I'm pleased for all of them. This will live in the memory of everyone in Cheltenham. As a Cheltenham man this means everything to me. It's going to take time to sink in that we are in the Football League and I'm just going to enjoy the moment, the euphoria of it all. I'm so pleased for all my family – my wife Tessa – for the backing they've given me and the belief they have had in me. They say behind every good man there's a good woman. I think I'm a good man, at least that's what 6,000 people told me tonight! My two daughters haven't had a dad for four years, including the time I was manager of Irish club Sligo Rovers, and we're going to put that right, that's for sure.

When the final whistle blew, Cotterill collapsed to his knees on the edge of the pitch. He was mobbed by well-wishers before taking the applause of the crowds which flooded onto the pitch.

Cheltenham Town: Book, Duff, Banks, Brough, Freeman, Victory, Howells, Bloomer, Norton, Grayson, Bailey (Knight 85). Subs not used: Yates, Eaton.
Yeovil Town: Pennock, Piper (Simpson 69), Fishlock, Brown, Steele, Cousins, Chandler, Hayfield, Smith (Pounder 90), Patmore, Pickard (Keeling 76).
Referee: A. Penn (Kingswinford).
Attendance: 6,150.

Match 28: Mansfield Town v. Cheltenham Town

Nationwide League Division Three
Saturday 7 August 1999, Field Mill
Mansfield Town 0
Cheltenham Town 1 (Grayson 64)

Neil Grayson's booming header earned Cheltenham Town their first win as a Football League club at Mansfield Town's Field Mill. It was somewhat fitting that Grayson scored the landmark goal after the all-action forward's goals had propelled the Robins to the Nationwide Conference title the previous year. It was important that manager Steve Cotterill's side bounced back from their 2–0 opening day defeat at Rochdale a week earlier, when the Lancashire side were comfortable winners to spoil Cheltenham's big day.

Cotterill named the same side that had performed admirably in the midweek Worthington League Cup defeat at Norwich City, and Cheltenham faced dangerous right winger Lee Williams who was to become a Robins player two seasons later. Cheltenham-born Martin Devaney, aged twenty, made his first Football League start on the left wing. Devaney had agreed a two-year deal with the club the previous week after being released by Coventry City.

Mansfield, who had suffered a 6–0 opening day defeat by Brighton, looked like a useful side, but the Robins back line of Neil Howarth, Chris Banks, Mark Freeman and Jamie Victory held firm. The Stags, with several young, new players who were getting to know each other, were not as good a team as Rochdale, but they still managed to carve more chances than Cheltenham during the first twenty minutes. Goalkeeper Steve Book twice showed signs of nerves in that time, when he and Neil Howarth left the ball for each other and then he was slow to move out for a long punt which Mark Freeman kicked away from the experienced Tony Lormor. Headers by Lee Peacock and Lormor hit Antony Griffin and Neil Howarth respectively before Cheltenham forced their way into Mansfield's half and produced their first positive move. Jamie Victory and Martin Devaney made their way down the left until Victory got clear and rolled a cross into the path of Grayson, whose shot hit central defender David Linighan on its way for a corner. Lormor, an old-fashioned centre-forward, shot high from ten yards after twenty-six minutes and headed a Williams free-kick over the bar with almost as much power as Grayson was to produce later.

Cheltenham had a good fifteen minutes in heavy rain, although Victory's foot had to cut out a shot by Peacock. Midfielder David Kerr, sent off in the Brighton defeat, was lucky to get away with a talking-to after he tripped Hugh McAuley in the forty-fourth minute. Howarth, whose brother Lee used to play for Mansfield, was not so lucky in the fifty-fifth minute when he was cautioned for clattering full-back Andy Roscoe near the touchline.

Mansfield were having their best spell at that time and in the next few minutes a shot by Wayne Thomas went out off Chris Banks' back, Neil Richardson headed over the bar and Lormor and Roscoe both had shots blocked. Cheltenham's central midfield duo of Lee Howells and Mark Yates were outstanding as the Robins were forced to soak up pressure and hit their opponents on the break.

The goal arrived after sixty-four minutes and was a classic piece of counter-attacking. Mansfield had been on top, but from a Stags corner Hugh McAuley cleared and found Antony Griffin on the left. Griffin had acres of space to charge down the flank and upon reaching the byline, he switched onto his favoured right foot. He had time to deliver a teasing cross, which Grayson met with perfection to beat Barry Richardson with the most powerful of headers. Cheltenham held on to the lead with a little help from an excellent, slap-away save by Steve Book from a snap cross-shot by

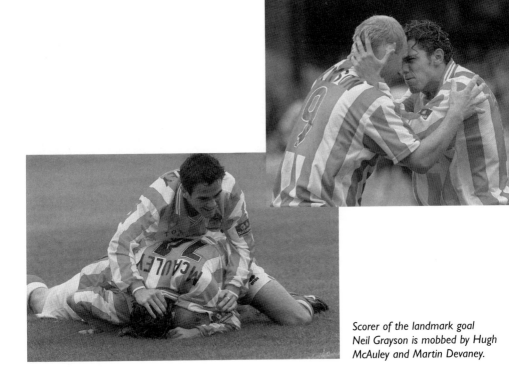

*Scorer of the landmark goal
Neil Grayson is mobbed by Hugh
McAuley and Martin Devaney.*

substitute Michael Boulding ten minutes from the end. Boulding almost joined Cheltenham in the summer of 2008 along with his brother Rory, but he chose to sign for Bradford City after a late change of heart.

Book was then forced into the save of the match from his own centre-half, as the outstanding Freeman almost deflected a long ball into his own net. Neil Richardson and Lormor also came close for the home side, but some heroic defending in the sodden conditions gave Cheltenham their historic win and the players and fans celebrated as if they had won the league when the final whistle was blown. Cotterill said, 'We're obviously delighted with the first win. It was important to get off the mark as soon as possible and we've now got that hurdle out of the way. This was a difficult game in difficult conditions, but we defended very well and took our chance when it came along. It was a good battle. Mansfield may have lost both their games, but they're not a bad side and we're chuffed with the result.' The win lifted Cheltenham to fifteenth place in the standings and pinned Mansfield, who had conceded seven and scored none, to the bottom. Cheltenham went on to win their next two matches against Hull City and Hartlepool United to ride high in the early days of their league life before suffering a slump in form from which they recovered to almost reach the play-offs at the end of their debut season among the élite ninety-two.

Mansfield Town: Richardson, Hassell, Roscoe, Kerr, Richardson, Linighan, Williams, Thomas (Blake 71), Lormor (Boulding 78), Peacock, Tallon, (Allardyce 83). Subs not used: Tye, Sisson,
Cheltenham Town: Book, Howarth, Banks, Freeman, Victory, Griffin, Yates, Howells, Devaney (Bloomer 85), McAuley (Watkins 70), Grayson. Subs not used: Duff, Brough, Higgs.
Referee: R. Pearson (Peterlee).
Attendance: 2,348.

MATCH 29: CHELTENHAM TOWN V. NORWICH CITY

Worthington Cup First Round second leg
Tuesday 24 August 1999, Whaddon Road
Cheltenham Town 2 (Grayson 47 pen, Victory 70)
Norwich City 1 (L. Marshall 100)

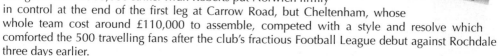

Cheltenham Town's first taste of Football League Cup action was a two-legged affair with Norwich City which illustrated how far the Robins had progressed in a short period of time. The Canaries won the competition in 1962 and 1985 and were runners-up in 1973 and 1975. While they were defeating Bayern Munich at the Olympic Stadium in the UEFA Cup in October 1993, Cheltenham needed extra-time to see off Weston-super-Mare in the first round of the Southern League Cup. However, six years later, manager Steve Cotterill's Cheltenham gave Norwich an almighty scare. Two first-half goals from £900,000 striker Iwan Roberts put Norwich firmly in control at the end of the first leg at Carrow Road, but Cheltenham, whose whole team cost around £110,000 to assemble, competed with a style and resolve which comforted the 500 travelling fans after the club's fractious Football League debut against Rochdale three days earlier.

Roberts, 6ft 3ins, headed the first goal from Phil Mulryne's cross in the fifteenth minute and he was slipped clear by Paul Dalglish for the second eight minutes before half-time Cheltenham-born Martin Devaney, signed a week earlier after being released by Coventry City, had an excellent first full game for Cheltenham, asserting himself on the left wing. Neil Grayson, the outstanding Mark Yates and Jamie Victory also nearly scored to reduce the deficit, but Norwich held onto their two-goal advantage going into the second leg.

The first leg attracted the fourth highest crowd ever to witness a match involving Cheltenham Town, after the 21,000 that saw them play an FA Cup tie at Hull City in 1947, the 16,500 for an FA Cup clash at Reading in 1950 and the 26,837 that watched the FA Umbro Trophy Final at Wembley in 1998. Bruce Rioch's side were joint bottom of Division One as they visited Cheltenham for the first time, while the Robins had won two in a row to climb to ninth in the early Division Three standings. Rioch, capped twenty-four times for Scotland, was one of the few managers who wrote to congratulate Cheltenham on winning the Nationwide Conference the previous season. However, he was left stunned as the incredible happened on a night of magic at Whaddon Road.

Goals from Neil Grayson, from the penalty spot, and Victory were not enough to send Cheltenham into the second round. Their hearts were broken by Lee Marshall's goal in extra-time, giving Norwich a 3–2 aggregate victory, but the glory went to Cheltenham, who surpassed anything they had done in a single game in their history. The Grayson penalty after forty-seven minutes and Victory's headed goal from a corner twelve minutes later gave the game a sharpness and Cheltenham an edge which few would have imagined possible. They matched Norwich across the pitch with almost unreal efficiency and there was no question which side were more worried as the end of the normal time approached. However, Norwich survived to score the goal, which took them through to a second-round tie against Fulham, in the tenth minute of extra-time. Roberts broke quickly away and crossed to the far post for Marshall to turn in, despite shouts for offside from Cheltenham.

It was a chilling end to a scintillating night and Cheltenham could take pride from beating a Division One club fair and square, if only over half a tie. They did it despite losing the increasingly influential Yates with a hamstring pull after only ten minutes and sending out youngster Michael Jackson, untried at the level. Jackson slotted straight in and had not been on the pitch very long when he made goalkeeper Andy Marshall fly with an angled shot from twenty yards which dropped just over the bar. He was then booked in the twenty-second minute for a tough challenge and at the time Norwich were still trying to absorb the fact that Cheltenham intended to give them a game.

Neil Grayson celebrates.

Mark Yates on the charge.

Mulryne, a £500,000 buy from Manchester United, followed Jackson into the book on the half-hour for dissent and by half-time both goalkeepers had to drop on dives, from Cedric Anselin and Devaney. If the first half suggested that confident Cheltenham had nothing to fear, the second half proved it. It had been going only two minutes when Antony Griffin sprinted into the box and fell as Craig Fleming closed in. A penalty was given and Grayson hit it hard and wide of Andy Marshall. Between then and Victory's goal, forward Hugh McAuley had an easy chance to score when he closed on Griffin's rolled pass from the right and met it six yards out after it had passed Andy Marshall. It seemed that all McAuley had to do was touch it straight, but he did not steer the ball firmly enough and it trickled wide.

Cheltenham kept going at Norwich with effective, sometimes intricate, passing and it led eventually to a corner which Devaney took. Victory jumped highest and goalkeeper Marshall was beaten high in his left corner. Suddenly the tie was 2–2 with twenty minutes to go, and the way Cheltenham were playing, a major upset was not only possible, but likely. Roberts shot as he fell and Steve Book claimed it on his chest and then tipped over a shot by Mulryne, but Norwich shots were isolated events until substitute Jean Yves de Blasiis gave Book a save in the first half of extra-time. The goal that mattered so much to them was due to Roberts' alertness and ability to turn clear of a defence. As de Blasiis passed, he moved and nobody got near him on his journey to the goal line. Once there he steered it across to the far post, where Marshall was waiting to stretch and push it in. Bob Bloomer and Dale Watkins replaced Devaney and McAuley for the last fifteen minutes, but there was no more magic; there had been enough of that already. Rioch was quick to praise the efforts of Cheltenham, who stunned Norwich in the same competition three years later.

Cheltenham Town: Book, Howarth, Freeman, Banks, Victory, Griffin, Yates (Jackson 10), Howells, Devaney (Bloomer 105), Grayson, McAuley (Watkins 105). Subs not used: Brough, Higgs.
Norwich City: A. Marshall, Sutch, Mackay, Fleming, Wilson, Dalglish (Diop 83), Anselin (de Blasiis 69), Mulryne, L. Marshall, Llewellyn, Roberts. Subs not used: Green, Coote, Fuglestad.
Referee: P. Dowd (Stoke-on-Trent).
Attendance: 4,203

Match 30: Cheltenham Town v. Barnet

Nationwide League Division Three
Saturday 2 December 2000, Whaddon Road
Cheltenham Town 4 (McAuley 9, 36, Alsop 62, 89)
Barnet 3 (Currie 25, Cottee 27, Riza 60)

Robins boss Steve Cotterill described this match as the kind that gave him grey hairs and although neither manager would have been happy with the defending on display, it was a terrific spectacle for the Whaddon Road crowd. Barnet had recorded a double over the Robins the previous season and were led by former West Ham and Everton goal machine Tony Cottee, who was player-manager of the London outfit. Barnet had made the national headlines when they'd appointed Cottee a month earlier. He replaced experienced boss John Still, who took Maidstone United into the Football league before managing Peterborough United. Still was promoted to Football Director, while Cottee, who also played for England, was named player-manager. Cottee watched from the sidelines for his first game at the club – a goalless draw at Rochdale, but made a fairytale start to his spell as player-manager, scoring the first goal in a spectacular 7–0 thrashing of Blackpool at Underhill.

The Bees completed a win double over Cheltenham during the 1999/2000 season, winning 2–1 at Whaddon Road and 3–2 at Underhill. Both Cheltenham and Barnet were in contention for promotion during the first half of the following campaign and it was Cheltenham who made an early breakthrough. A long throw from Mike Duff was flicked on by big centre-half Mark Freeman. Bees' goalkeeper Danny Naisbitt saved well from Mark Yates, who had connected powerfully with the flick on, but Hugh McAuley was on hand to finish clinically from the rebound.

Darren Currie always seemed to impress when he came up against Cheltenham and the tricky winger levelled the scores after twenty-five minutes. Currie's mazy dribble took him past Yates and Lee Howells before his low shot beat Steve Book at the near post. Cottee then showed his class with a superb turn and shot from the edge of the area to give his side the lead. Both sides were committed to attack and it was no surprise when another goal hit the back of the net to leave the scores all square going into the break. Yates' cross from the right was flicked on by towering striker Julian Alsop and McAuley was waiting at the far post again to beat Naisbitt from twelve yards.

Cottee continued to cause the home defence problems in the second half and his measured lob was forced over the line by Riza, who slid in ahead of the defender. However, Barnet's lead only lasted for two minutes as Naisbitt flapped at a Howells cross and the ball fell to Alsop to roll home into an empty net. Mark Arber was dismissed for two cautions and a remarkable game then took another twist as the seventh and final goal was scored. Both sides had chances to seal all three points but Alsop, who had been an aerial threat throughout, completed his brace and at the same time clinched a last-gasp win for Cheltenham. The winner arrived with one minute remaining and it was another close-range finish for Alsop, who prodded home after Barnet had failed to deal with a McAuley corner.

The three points nudged Cheltenham up to sixth in the table with thirty-four points, moving them ahead of Scunthorpe United, who lost 1–0 at home to improving Hull City. Barnet's season took an alarming turn for the worse and they ended up returning to the Conference after a miserable second half to their campaign.

After the game, Cotterill said, 'What a game it was. I'm getting a bit carried away with myself. It was an unbelievable advert for Division Three and if people didn't enjoy themselves today, I don't

Julian Alsop salutes the Whaddon Road crowd after scoring against Barnet.

know when they will. We deserved to win, and the only downside was that they got three goals against the run of play.'

Cheltenham suffered a nightmare run of serious injuries and saw their play-off hopes fade in the final weeks of a tough season for Cotterill's men. Cotterill made an approach to sign Cottee in the summer of 2001 as he attempted to add a twenty-goals-a-season player to his squad. He made an offer to the thirty-five-year-old, who averaged a goal every two and a bit games when he played at the highest level. Cottee was a free agent after leaving Barnet and making two appearances for Millwall, claiming the distinction of playing in all four divisions during a single season. He had started the season with top flight club Leicester before a brief spell with Norwich City in Division One. After seriously considering Cotterill's offer, Cottee opted to turn it down as he had a young family who were settled in Essex and he was reluctant to move away for a year. Cotterill eventually signed Tony Naylor, who was a revelation up front alongside Julian Alsop, forming the famed 'little and large' partnership that fired Cheltenham to promotion in 2002.

Cheltenham Town: Book, Griffin, Freeman, Banks, McCann, Duff, Yates, Howells, McAuley, Alsop, Grayson (White 75). Subs not used: Bloomer, Milton, Devaney, Higgs.
Barnet: Naisbitt, Stockley, Goodhind, Arber, Sawyers, Currie, Doolan, Niven, Toms, Riza, (Gledhill 67), Cottee (Purser 83).
Referee: M.J. North (Dorset)
Attendance: 3,599

Match 31: Cheltenham Town v. Brighton & HA

Nationwide League Division Three
Saturday 17 February 2001, Whaddon Road
Cheltenham Town 3 (McCann 8, Alsop 11, Bloomer 70)
Brighton & HA 1 (Cullip 14)

The 2000/01 campaign was a very frustrating one for Cheltenham Town, but one of the highlights was a fantastic victory over eventual champions of Division Three, Brighton, at Whaddon Road. A run of incredibly bad luck had deprived Cheltenham of key men for long periods, with Jamie Victory and John Brough forced to spend virtually the whole season on the sidelines with knee injuries. There were times when Steve Cotterill was forced to field something close to a reserve side and despite a brave effort from a squad that was stretched to its limits, the play-offs were a step too far in the Robins' second season in the League. On their day however, they proved they were a match for anyone in the division, as high-flying Brighton learned. On-loan striker Chris Iwelumo, who was to progress to win international honours with Scotland, missed the game with a knee injury after scoring on his debut in a 2–1 defeat at Mansfield Town the previous Tuesday.

Cheltenham started as outsiders having lost their last five games, scoring only twice. They had lost to Hartlepool United, Shrewsbury Town, Hull City, Chesterfield and Mansfield in the run up to their Brighton test. The victory was all the more remarkable considering that Cheltenham were reduced to ten men after only twenty minutes. They had already given themselves a 2–1 lead by the time Lee Howells was shown his marching orders. The midfielder had already been cautioned, but was unfortunate to be sent off after Martin Devaney had gone in late on a Brighton defender. The referee gave the card to the wrong player and the decision was later overturned after a look at the video. Cheltenham had taken the lead after eight minutes through the on-loan Grant McCann, who drove a thirty-five-yard shot into the bottom right corner of Mark Cartwright's goal. It was the West Ham loan star's first goal for Cheltenham. Things were to get better for Cheltenham three minutes later when they added another against a shell-shocked Seagulls. Hugh McAuley's corner was flicked on by Richard Walker and towering striker Julian Alsop crashed home a header from close range. There was a real cup tie atmosphere inside Whaddon Road, but Brighton pulled a goal back three minutes later in what was a very open game with chances aplenty at both ends. Danny Cullip headed in Paul Watson's free-kick to pull his side back into contention.

Steve Book was on top form to maintain the Robins' lead as the promotion-chasing visitors began to show their class and make their extra man tell. Book denied Anthony Philip David Terry Frank Donald Stanley Gerry Gordon Stephen James Oatway (known to his friends as simply 'Charlie'!), and also made smart stops from Darren Freeman and Watson. After soaking up all Bobby Zamora and Co. could throw at them, Cheltenham hit Brighton on the break and with twenty minutes left, one of the most popular goals ever seen at Whaddon Road was scored. Substitute Bob Bloomer, already a living legend at the club, picked up the ball thirty-five yards from goal on the right wing. He held it up before cutting inside onto his supposedly weaker left side. Bloomer, in his farewell season, then unleashed a curling left-foot shot which nestled perfectly inside the far post. He celebrated as if Cheltenham had won the FA Cup and his jubilant lap of honour will live long in the memory. It was Bloomer's first Football League goal for Cheltenham and his first strike since his wonder goal against Halifax Town in the club's penultimate season outside the League, in 1997. Bloomer did not score in his twenty-two games for Bristol Rovers, but he did hit fifteen in 141 for Chesterfield. He had only been on the field for six minutes after replacing Devaney before he struck in the seventieth minute. It was a question of patience rewarded because Bloomer was on the substitutes' bench for all but the first three of Cheltenham's forty-six Division Three matches the previous season. He started the historic first against Rochdale, which ended in a 2–0 defeat. The Brighton game was his twenty-first substitute appearance that season, compensated for by five starts.

After Bloomer's stunner, Book had more work to do before the win was assured, denying the dangerous Zamora, but the agile 'keeper would not be beaten again. The famous win was something to remember from a difficult season for Steve Cotterill's decimated squad. 'Brighton are a good side and well up there, and to beat them with twelve men would have been great, but with ten it was fantastic,' Cotterill said.

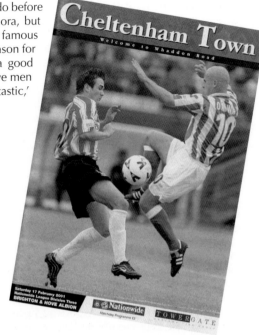

Cheltenham Town: Book, Griffin, Walker, Howarth, M. Freeman, McCann, Howells, Yates, Devaney, McAuley, Alsop. Subs used: Bloomer, White.
Brighton & HA: Cartwright, Watson, Mayo, Crosby, Cullip, Wicks, D. Freeman, Oatway, Rogers, Zamora, Carpenter. Subs used: Hart, Brooker, Jones.
Referee: R. Beeby (Northamptonshire).
Attendance: 4,533.

MATCH 32: CHELTENHAM TOWN V. CARDIFF CITY

Nationwide League Division Three
1 April 2001, Whaddon Road
Cheltenham Town 3 (Grayson 37, 41, 49)
Cardiff City 1 (Young 6)

Neil Grayson hit the fifth hat-trick of his career and his first for Cheltenham Town to sink big-spending Cardiff City and keep the Robins' Nationwide League Division Three play-off hopes alive in 2001. The never-say-die attitude of Grayson typified the performance of Steve Cotterill's side after they had fallen behind. To concede an early goal against one of the biggest clubs with a fine pedigree was the last thing Cheltenham, who moved into the final play-off spot, needed. They struggled to get the measure of Cardiff for the first thirty minutes, when the automatic promotion-seeking Welsh club's expensive players promised a salutary lesson to Cheltenham's honest labourers. It threatened to boil up into another ugly game, after the emotions of the two matches between the clubs at Ninian Park in December when Cheltenham had Julian Alsop and Michael Duff sent off, and Leo Fortune-West, who was substituted near the end after being well shackled, was booked for taking a kick at Mark Sertori.

Grayson was cautioned for pushing in the thirtieth minute, but the game began to turn ten minutes before half-time when a cross by Duff led to a goal. Midfielder Mark Yates had the first stab when the ball dropped in front of him with players all around trying to scramble the ball away. His shot was diverted to his left and Grayson needed no second bidding. His rasping shot soared into the far corner to give Cheltenham a big lift, which became a bigger one when he scored again five minutes later with a dipping near-post header from midfielder Russell Milton's corner. The corner had been forced by Charlie MacDonald, who turned David Hughes and whacked a shot which was bound for the far corner of goal before goalkeeper Mark Walton got an arm to it. MacDonald, on loan from Charlton Athletic, played a big part in the third goal. It was from his clever pass that Grayson badgered Rhys Weston into losing it. Grayson slid in to tackle Weston and wriggled and ferreted before the ball squeezed goalside on Weston, leaving Grayson to stand up, move forward and slide his left-foot shot past Walton. It was an outrageous goal, born entirely of Grayson's appetite.

Although they had a strong last twenty minutes, Cardiff never looked like scoring again against a Cheltenham side which used a 3-5-2 formation, with Chris Banks, Sertori and Richard Walker the rocks at the back. That they made no impact was nothing to do with Andy Legg or Josh Low, both of whom looked to be playing below their standard. Legg's long throws made Greg Goodridge's look like gentle lobs and Low's runs on the right deserved to lead to better.

There was a standing ovation for Grayson when he was replaced, in the ninetieth minute, by Martin Devaney, and another for the team when they walked off. Grayson, thirty-six, had a series of problems with injuries that season yet his treble earned him a career-best for a Football League season. He had started only seventeen Division Three games, but the hat-trick took him to eleven League goals for the season. He had scored two in cup competitions. The best the Chesterfield-based striker had done before was twelve, when he was at Northampton, and the previous season he got ten for Cheltenham. He scored one hat-trick for Boston and three at Northampton. One of the ones he had at Northampton was against Hartlepool and he scored it in four minutes, two just before half-time and one just after. Two of his goals then were shots and one a header, which makes it very similar to his achievement against Cardiff. He also scored with two shots and a header, and two of his goals were scored just before half-time, in the thirty-sixth and forty-first minutes, with the other following in the forty-ninth. For a man who broke an ankle in the second match of the season

Neil Grayson climbs highest to head his second goal.

and had since been out with a pulled hamstring and two more kicks on the ankle, it was a sweet time. He left the pitch in tears when his ankle last went, in the 1–0 defeat by Hull City on 3 February, but the tears were replaced by a beam against Cardiff. 'It's nice to be back playing again, and it's great to score three in such a big game, but the result was the most important thing for us,' he said. 'I just want to keep playing as long as I can. My contract's up at the end of the season but I feel now as I did when I was thirty. When I had the broken ankle at the beginning of the season, I was beginning to worry if I would lose my speed. I don't think I have, but perhaps the others are getting quicker!' Manager Steve Cotterill said there were people who had questioned the wisdom of signing a thirty-three-year-old when he paid Hereford United £10,000 for Grayson in March 1998. 'You have only so many games in your legs and Neil is cherishing every game,' Cotterill said. 'Taking nothing away from him, but it was a team performance today. Charlie MacDonald did very well and so did Julian Alsop when he went on in the second half.' MacDonald, in his fourth game for the club after joining on a month's loan from Charlton Athletic, had his best game for Cheltenham. His pass helped to set Grayson up for his hat-trick goal and it was his shot which produced the corner from which Grayson nodded in his second.

It was not only at the front that Cheltenham were impressive. Cotterill's decision to play a 3-5-2 formation with Chris Banks flanked by Richard Walker and Sertori at the heart of the defence, overwhelmed Cardiff's big 6ft 4in striker Leo Fortune-West. 'In terms of the physical contest, we're not normally found wanting in that area but we produced some big bits of quality as well,' said Cotterill.

Cheltenham Town: Book, Walker, Banks, Sertori, McCann, Milton, Yates, Howells, Duff, MacDonald (Alsop 53), Grayson. Subs not used: Griffin, Higgs, McAuley,
Cardiff City: Walton, Gabbidon, Weston, Hughes (Giles 63), Legg, Boland, Young, Bowen (Brayson 69), Earnshaw, Low, Fortune-West (Collins 83). Subs not used: Evans, Muggleton,
Referee: C.J. Foy (Merseyside).
Attendance: 5,139.

Match 33: Cheltenham Town v. Oldham Athletic

FA Cup Third Round
Saturday 6 January 2002, Whaddon Road
Cheltenham Town 2 (Naylor 25, 60)
Oldham Athletic 1 (Eyres 43)

Cheltenham Town caused an FA Cup upset and made it through to the fourth round for the first time in their history with a deserved victory over League One high-flyers Oldham Athletic. With wins over non-league outfits Kettering Town and Hinckley United in the earlier rounds, League Two Cheltenham entertained the former Premiership club in fine form after what had been a productive Christmas period for Steve Cotterill's promotion-chasing side. They went into the game high on confidence, undefeated in six matches and beaten only three times in twenty-three games in all competitions.

Oldham had reached the semi-finals of the Cup in 1913, 1990 and 1994, and were beaten by Manchester United both times in the 1990s. They lost both ties in a replay and the Boundary Park club also reached the final of the League Cup in 1990, when they lost 1–0 to Nottingham Forest. They were guided into the top flight by Joe Royle and were in the Premiership in 1993/94, their second and last season.

The first goal attempt of the match was by Cheltenham winger Lee Williams, hungry for another after his match-winning strike at Torquay United on New Year's Day. Former Mansfield Town man Williams cut in from the right, where he had a good game, and shot through several bodies but not with enough power to bother goalkeeper Gary Kelly. Julian Alsop fired long and low past a post and soon forced Lee Duxbury into an ungainly headed clearance from in front of his own goalkeeper. In the seventeenth minute, left side midfielder Russell Milton's twenty-yard shot flew over the bar.

It was diminutive forward Tony Naylor who opened the scoring after twenty-five minutes, having passed a fitness test on the morning of the game. His strike partner in crime, Alsop, flicked on a goal kick from Steve Book and Naylor rounded defender Scott McNiven before slotting the ball in at the near post from fifteen yards. Naylor's strike still prompted no major assault by Oldham, whose first real chance was dropped upon by Book after Paul Murray had got to the line and cut it back for striker John Eyre.

Despite struggling for much of the first half, Oldham equalised two minutes before the break through David Eyres. Left-sided Eyres, who was approaching his thirty-eighth birthday, was Oldham's dominant force when they went forward. Defender Darren Sheridan, brother of former Latics player and manager John, who also played, supplied John Eyre down the right flank and his cross was finished by Eyres from close range to put the Latics back in the tie. Eyres' goal was something of a kick in the teeth for Cheltenham and all their effort, but it turned out not to be as ominous as it appeared.

Cheltenham came out for the second half full of confidence, and Naylor and the impressive Williams saw efforts blocked as Cheltenham belied the difference in divisions between the two clubs. The home side were rewarded for their almost constant pressure with an hour gone as Naylor claimed his second goal of the afternoon. Naylor's 5ft 4in frame was at the far post when a curling cross by right side midfielder Lee Williams floated over on the hour, and his header went inside the post off the body of central defender Stuart Balmer. Naylor shot off towards the new Wyman's Road stand, jumping and kicking and generally looking as though he knew they would go on to set up a tie against Burnley at Whaddon Road and that the goal meant a great deal to him. Naylor's presence in the starting line-up had been in doubt all week after he had picked up a knee injury in the 2–2 Nationwide League division three draw with Swansea City the previous Saturday which caused him to miss the 1–0 win at Torquay's Plainmoor. Naylor was still feeling some pain in his knee hours before the game but decided to take a gamble – and how it paid off, for him and for Cheltenham. The goals were Naylor's eleventh and twelfth goals of the season, seven of them in his previous five games.

Right: Chris Banks and Michael Duff hoist Tony Naylor aloft.

Far right: Naylor wheels away in delight after netting against Oldham.

The ball continued to stay on the ground for the bulk of the game as Cheltenham more than matched the Latics pass for pass and move for move. Oldham midfielder Darren Sheridan was booked in the seventy-third minute and two minutes later Alsop was also cautioned for a foul on Balmer as Oldham remained subdued.

The Robins back four of Antony Griffin, Jamie Victory, Chris Banks and Michael Duff defended solidly throughout and Oldham were reduced to ten men five minutes before the final whistle. Sheridan was sent off for a second caution, but there was already the clear impression that this was going to be Cheltenham's day. Naylor would have had a hat-trick but for a dramatic, fisted punch off his line by Kelly five minutes from the end. When the former Port Vale man was taken off a minute from the end, Naylor deserved every decibel of the ovation he was given after he had made it five goals in three cup ties that season (two against Kettering Town and one against Hinckley United). So, when the game ended, did the rest of the players. The most

Robins boss Steve Cotterill at the final whistle with Naylor behind.

impressive part of Cheltenham's triumph, only their third over a Football League club in the FA Cup, was that they won on merit and not by slam-banging Oldham into submission. A healthy crowd had witnessed a groundbreaking result for the Robins. They scooped £50,000 in prize money and were paired with Championship club Burnley in round four.

Cheltenham Town: Book, Griffin, M. Duff, Banks, Victory, Williams, Yates, Howells, Milton, Naylor (Grayson 90), Alsop. Subs not used: Brough, Higgs, Devaney, Howarth.
Oldham Athletic: Kelly, McNiven (Baudet 68), Beharall, Balmer, Murray, Duxbury, J. Sheridan, D. Sheridan, Eyre (Tipton 68), Smart (Dudley 74), Eyres. Subs not used: Hardy, Haining.
Referee: M.J. Brandwood (Staffordshire).
Attendance: 5,801.

MATCH 34: CHELTENHAM TOWN V. BURNLEY

FA Cup Fourth Round
Sunday 27 January 2002, Whaddon Road
Cheltenham Town 2 (Milton 23, Alsop 27)
Burnley 1 (A. Moore 29)

The managerial reign of Steve Cotterill reached a new high when his side rewrote the record books yet again, beating First Division outfit Burnley and reaching the fourth round of the FA Cup for the first time. Burnley were riding high and looked to be genuine contenders for promotion to the Premiership, but over 7,000 fans packed into Whaddon Road – the biggest crowd since the 1956 FA Cup tie with Reading – anticipating an upset; they were not disappointed. The match was switched to a Sunday, due to a clash with a major race meeting at the Prestbury Park, with a 1 p.m. kick-off. Cheltenham's strike pairing of Julian Alsop and Tony Naylor already had twenty-nine goals between them before one of the highest profile matches the club had ever taken part in. The match was one that Robins midfielder Mark Yates had been looking forward to since he left Burnley in 1993. Defender Neil Howarth, named among the substitutes, was also a former Burnley player.

Burnley were one of the great clubs of the land half a century earlier, when Cheltenham were struggling to survive in the modest world of the Southern League, where they spent fifty years. On this occasion, it was virtually impossible to tell which side was from Division One and which from the Football League's basement. Cheltenham took the game to Burnley right from the off and could have been two goals up before Russell Milton's sweetly struck shot, following a clever free-kick move, flew past Luigi Cennamo. Alsop had headed a Jamie Victory cross over the bar before Victory himself shot agonisingly wide, after a wonderful move involving Milton and the irrepressible Tony Naylor. Burnley 'keeper Nik Michopoulos left the field of play after seventeen minutes to be replaced by the inexperienced Cennamo, on-loan from Greek side Olympiakos. Cennamo's first real action was to pick the ball out of his goal, after Milton's effort beat the wall and hit the back of the net after twenty-three minutes. Shell-shocked Burnley found themselves two down barely three minutes later. Milton cut inside from out on the left flank and his right-footed cross was met by the unchallenged Alsop, who powered his header downwards and as it rose to hit the roof of the net, Whaddon Road erupted.

Burnley needed an immediate response and Alan Moore provided it after twenty-nine minutes. It was a fine goal from the left-footed midfielder. He broke through and as the Cheltenham defence stood off him, he was able to beat Steve Book and bring the stunned Clarets' fans back to life.

Naylor went off with a minor knee injury in the fifty-third minute and Neil Grayson went on to wreak his particular kind of havoc. For the last thirty minutes, Cheltenham snapped at ankles like terrier dogs and Burnley dodged and danced to avoid them. They went forward most of the time, but Alan Moore was the only player who looked like spoiling Cheltenham's great day. Book made one outstanding save, in the seventy-fourth minute, when he threw himself and flung out a hand to divert a skidding shot by Welsh international Gareth Taylor beyond the far post. Mark Yates, a late goal specialist, almost added to his collection, when he surged forward after first Alsop and then Grayson, had nodded the ball on, but he did not catch his volley right.

The biggest howl of the afternoon from the crowd was reserved for the moment when the fourth official raised a board indicating five minutes of time to be added on. Nobody in the 7,300 crowd knew how such a figure had been arrived at, but Cheltenham survived it and took their place in the last sixteen, where they would travel to promotion-seeking West Bromwich Albion. Skipper Chris

Above: Milton also set up Julian Alsop for goal number two.

Left: Russell Milton opened the scoring.

Banks was named man-of-the-match for a masterful performance at the back for Cheltenham. After the game, Cotterill said:

> To beat Oldham Athletic 2–1 in the last round was an unbelievable achievement and to get through again is a dream. The prize money for winning this round [£75,000] is massive to us and it will mean the chairman and directors don't have to worry so much about where the next penny is coming from. Russell Milton's goal was something we've worked on, although not this week. But as I said to him, we've been waiting for that goal to come along for the past twelve months. If it does beat the wall, it is a hard one for a goalkeeper to save.

Former Arsenal trainee Milton said, 'It's something you dream of, but to beat a club like Burnley is a great achievement for Cheltenham Town. We had to get straight at them kicking downhill and with the wind in our favour in the first half and for us to go two goals up made it a lot harder for them. As soon as we were awarded the free-kick I fancied it. I just had to make sure I hit the target and I caught their goalkeeper a bit cold, too.' Cotterill, the man who masterminded Burnley's downfall at Whaddon Road, went on to join the Clarets as manager in the summer of 2004 and oversaw wins over Aston Villa in the League Cup and Liverpool in the FA Cup in his first season. The Clarets finished thirteenth in the Championship, and finished seventeenth a year later as Cotterill was forced to sell of some of his prized assets such as Ade Akinbiyi and Richard Chaplow. Cotterill eventually left Turf Moor in November 2007 by mutual consent after earning the title of longest-serving manager in the division, with three years and seven months' service.

Cheltenham Town: Book, Griffin, M. Duff, Banks, Victory, Williams, Yates, Howells, Milton, Alsop, Naylor (Grayson 53). Subs not used: Brough, Higgs, Devaney, Howarth.
Burnley: Michopoulos (Cennamo 17), West, Cox, Gnohere, Briscoe, Little (Branch 77), Ball, Grant, A. Moore, I. Moore (Maylett 84), Taylor. Subs not used: Cook, Armstrong.
Referee: A.N. Butler (Nottinghamshire).
Attendance: 7,300.

MATCH 35: WEST BROMWICH ALBION v. CHELTENHAM TOWN

FA Cup Fifth Round
Saturday 16 February 2002, The Hawthorns
West Bromwich Albion 1 (Dichio 64)
Cheltenham Town 0

Cheltenham Town's groundbreaking FA Cup run of 2001/02 took them through to the last sixteen for the first time and the last remaining Division Three club in the competition were drawn away at West Bromwich Albion. The Baggies, managed by Gary Megson, were riding high in their division and pushing for a place in the Premiership. The match was watched by the biggest crowd ever to assemble for a match involving Cheltenham Town, with 27,179 packed inside The Hawthorns with a quarter-final place at stake. Five years earlier, Cheltenham won 4–1 at Cambridge City in front of 227 fans in the Dr Marten's League. Steve Cotterill's Robins had progressed two stages further than ever before with wins over Kettering Town, Hinckley United, Oldham Athletic and Burnley. Cheltenham knew that something special would have to happen if they were still to be in the competition when the sixth round draw was made. They could hardly have done more trying to make that something special happen. They matched Albion, £2 million striker Jason Roberts and all, for just over an hour before Slovak right wing-back Igor Balis' cross was headed in by £1.25 million centre-forward Danny Dichio and the end of the dream was nigh.

Before that, in the first half, a penalty might have been given when Mark Yates' legs were caught just inside the Albion box by Phil Gilchrist. The midfielder fell, but referee Matt Messias showed no interest. Cheltenham could also consider themselves unlucky in the second half when midfielder Adam Chambers was responsible for one of the game's turning points. He was on the line to chest down a goal-bound header from Jamie Victory, who ran in from the left and across the Albion defence to meet a corner taken by Russell Milton in the fifty-sixth minute. What might have happened if that had gone in was anybody's guess. There would have been bedlam in the Smethwick End, where Cheltenham's 5,000 fans were, but instead, seven minutes later, they were silenced. Dichio's head had struck. The goal, ironically, was scored two minutes after Cheltenham manager Steve Cotterill had decided to shore up his defence by taking off striker Tony Naylor and midfielder Milton, replacing them with John Brough and Neil Grayson. Brough, in his second senior game since recovering from a serious knee operation sixteen months earlier, went on to make it five at the back and Grayson, who had played up front and on the left of the midfield that season, simply made as big a nuisance of himself as he could.

Just before Dichio's goal, goalkeeper Steve Book made a remarkable, two-fisted blocking save when he threw himself towards Roberts, whose pace and strength had taken him in close, despite the attentions of Antony Griffin. Cheltenham did have their moments and Yates, once a ball-boy at The Hawthorns, made ex-Robins loan goalkeeper Russell Hoult fly to tip over a left-foot shot from twenty yards, as Cheltenham pressed for the equaliser.

The most contentious moment of the match came in the twenty-second minute and might have seen Chris Banks sent off. Roberts, the first time his danger potential was seen, scorched deep into the Cheltenham half and approached Banks. Banks turned, but left his leg in the way of Roberts, who was floored thirty yards from goal. To Banks' relief, referee Messias decided it was not a clear scoring opportunity and Cheltenham's skipper escaped with a yellow card.

Most of the early West Bromwich threats were courtesy of Cheltenham giving them the ball. Milton had the first decent chance to give Cheltenham a shock advantage when a clearance by Larus Sigurdsson went straight to him and, with his less favoured right foot, he shot too quickly and too high.

Mark Yates gets stuck in at the Hawthorns.

Antony Griffin tackles Jason Roberts.

Despite the ceaseless promptings of midfielder Derek McInnes and the forward thrusts of Andrew Johnson, Albion were not able to pull Cheltenham out of their well-drilled shape. The left foot of Neil Clement rammed a shot through the wall, but past Book's left post from the free-kick which followed Banks' booking, but most of the play was in the midfield.

Cheltenham got close in the thirty-ninth minute when Yates charged forward for Naylor's low cross, but Hoult read it and beat him to it. At the other end, Chambers had a chance, but he put it straight at Book. Michael Duff later took responsibility for the goal, at the end of a week that saw him became Cheltenham's first full international when he went on for the last eight minutes of Northern Ireland's friendly against Poland in Cyprus.

Once Dichio's goal had gone in, Cheltenham had to go for glory. Martin Devaney went on for Lee Williams, but he could not make an impact and the Yates blast which Hoult tipped over was to be their last serious assault. Albion substitute Scott Dobie had a chance to kill off the tie ten minutes from the end, but he spooned badly high after Balis had got to the line and pulled it back. When the end came, Cheltenham knew they had far from let themselves down and took their bows for a sterling performance against a team fifty-four places above them in the league ladder. After the game Cotterill said, 'I was proud of the boys because they didn't freeze and we played some good stuff at times.' Megson was glowing in his praise of Cheltenham, 'They didn't look like a Division Three side to me and they've got a really good chance of going up. They've got a lot of experience, are well organised and work hard.' The cup run was worth around £350,000 to Cheltenham, who went on to win promotion via the play-offs at the Millennium Stadium with a 3–1 win over Rushden & Diamonds. The £375,000 gate receipts were the highest in West Brom's history. It was their thirteenth 1–0 win at the Hawthorns that season – another record.

West Bromwich Albion: Hoult, Sigurdsson, Moore (Butler 82), Gilchrist, Balis, McInnes, A. Chambers (Dobie 58), Johnson, Clement, Dichio, Roberts. Subs not used: Jensen, Butler, Fox, Jordao.
Cheltenham Town: Book, Griffin, M. Duff, Banks, Victory, Williams (Devaney 69), Yates, Howells, Milton (Brough 61), Alsop, Naylor (Grayson 61). Subs not used: Higgs, Howarth.
Referee: M.D. Massias (Yorkshire).
Attendance: 27,179.

MATCH 36: CHELTENHAM TOWN V. HARTLEPOOL UNITED

Nationwide League Division Three play-off semi-final, second leg
Tuesday 30 April 2002, Whaddon Road
Cheltenham Town 1 (Williams 26)
Hartlepool United 1 (Arnison 17)
(Cheltenham won 5–4 on pens)

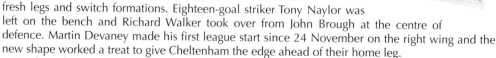

After narrowly missing out on automatic promotion on the final day of the season at Division Three champions Plymouth Argyle, Cheltenham Town overcame Hartlepool United over a two-legged play-off semi-final. There was nothing to choose between the sides in either match and even the decisive penalty stayed out by a hair's breadth. The first leg had ended all square, with Neil Grayson hitting a crucial equaliser for Cheltenham at Victoria Park. It was Grayson's first goal for seven months and it came in the eighty-ninth minute to change the tone of the contest. Martyn Lee charged down a clearance by Chris Westwood, who went on to play for Cheltenham during the 2008/09 season on loan from Peterborough United, and slipped the ball to Grayson, who did the rest. Grayson came on the left of a five-man midfield, as boss Steve Cotterill decided to use fresh legs and switch formations. Eighteen-goal striker Tony Naylor was left on the bench and Richard Walker took over from John Brough at the centre of defence. Martin Devaney made his first league start since 24 November on the right wing and the new shape worked a treat to give Cheltenham the edge ahead of their home leg.

Hartlepool, who climbed to seventh place by a run of five straight wins, were holding a lead earned by the head of Eifion Williams on the stroke of half-time. 'Pool then faced a marathon midweek trip down to Gloucestershire and manager Chris Turner's side started purposefully. Before the game, Cotterill appealed to fans to roar his side into the play-off final at Whaddon Road. Just as they had done in the first leg, Hartlepool took a first-half lead. Paul Smith's cross was headed out by Richard Walker, but it fell to wing-back Paul Arnison who drove home an unstoppable shot from twenty yards to stun Whaddon Road. Arnison was cautioned for spending too long celebrating his goal and Cheltenham had to battle for long spells to keep out the visitors. The setback startled Cheltenham into life and after trailing for nine minutes, Lee Williams scored one of the goals of the season to put the Robins back on level terms. Williams had been a revelation on the right side of midfield following his move from Mansfield earlier in the season. The former Aston Villa youngster cut inside and thundered in a left-foot shot that cannoned in off the cross bar, leaving Anthony Williams with no chance whatsoever.

Just after Williams' goal for Cheltenham, former Southampton and Bradford City striker Gordon Watson side-footed high and shots by Eifion Williams and midfielder Darrell Clarke were deflected for corners as it stayed uncomfortable for Cheltenham. They had a bright moment when Williams touched a free-kick back to Russell Milton, whose twenty-yard drive speared an inch past the far post. However, it was Hartlepool who continued to play the aggressive football. Steve Book dropped on a shot by Paul Stephenson and Hartlepool forward Williams was cautioned for sliding late into the goalkeeper and there was no let-up from Hartlepool after half-time. The bullish runs on the left of Paul Smith were a constant pressure and Clarke missed badly in the fifty-eighth minute, when he moved onto Watson's pass at speed and lifted the ball over from eight yards.

Cheltenham picked up on the hour and a flurry of corners preceded their most open chance so far, when Williams' right-wing centre was headed past the far post by Naylor. Cotterill threw on Grayson and Devaney in the seventy-sixth minute and Lee replaced Milton ten minutes later. Hartlepool substitute Kevin Henderson, on for Williams, who scored the first-leg goal for Hartlepool,

Steve Book and Julian Alsop.

Book and Russell Milton look forward to the play-off final ahead.

dived to head at Book and in the ninetieth minute Michael Duff was close with a header at the back post. The thirty minutes of extra-time was a tight, nervy affair, with Grayson heading high from Lee's free-kick. Cheltenham were penned in front of their own goal for most of the second period, but Hartlepool could not break them down. It was no surprise when the match finished with honours even and a shoot-out was necessary to separate the two teams. Grayson was first up for Cotterill's side and the left-footer made no mistake. Paul Smith for 'Pool and Cheltenham's Lee, on-loan from Wycombe, converted, before Paul Stephenson blazed his shot over the bar to give the Robins an advantage. Skipper Mark Yates made no mistake and Arnison was on target for the visitors. Duff then missed for Cheltenham and after Kevin Henderson and John Finnigan had both found the net, the shoot-out moved into sudden death. Top scorer Julian Alsop calmly stepped up, slotted home and put the pressure on Hartlepool's Richie Humphreys who had to score to keep his side in with a chance of making the Millennium Stadium final. Humphreys' effort crashed against the bar, hit Book and hit a post, before finally rebounding to safety.

After a few seconds of disbelief, the celebrations began – Cheltenham had reached the final of the play-offs in only their third season in the Football League. Cotterill said, 'It was a tense, nervous game and we were not at our best. Still, there have been many occasions when we have not got our rewards. We should have got automatic promotion, and we could have beaten Darlington 7–1 if their goalkeeper had not had such a great game.' That match had ended 0–0 at Whaddon Road on 23 January. Cotterill added, 'We're still aiming for that promotion place, that over the course of the season, we deserve. I feel a little bit for Hartlepool. In fact, I really felt for them and for their manager, Chris Turner. They've been magnificent all season as well.'

Cheltenham Town: Book, M. Duff, Victory, Yates, Milton (M. Lee 85), Griffin, Walker, Alsop, Naylor (Grayson 76), L. Williams (Devaney 76), Finnigan.
Hartlepool United: A. Williams, Barron, G. Lee, Westwood, Arnison, Smith, Stephenson, Humphreys, Clarke, Watson, E. Williams (Henderson 78).
Referee: A.R. Hall (Herts).
Attendance: 7,165.

MATCH 37: CHELTENHAM TOWN V. RUSHDEN & DIAMONDS

Nationwide League Division Three play-off final
Monday 6 May 2002, Millennium Stadium
Cheltenham Town 3 (Devaney 27,
Alsop 49, Finnigan 80)
Rushden & Diamonds 1 (Hall 28)

Cheltenham Town secured promotion for the first time as a Football League club with a fantastic performance at Cardiff's Millennium Stadium against old foes Rushden & Diamonds. After a nail-biting penalty shoot-out semi-final victory over Hartlepool United, Steve Cotterill's men earned the right to face the Diamonds in the showpiece play-off final after they had defeated Rochdale over two legs in their semi. Cotterill already knew it was to be the last match of his incredible managerial reign, which saw the club climb from the Southern League to the verge of claiming a place in the third tier of English football for the first time, within five years. Once again the whole town unified in support of their progressive club. Even staff at Gianni Ristorante in Royal Well Place rolled their sleeves up and cooked a special edition red and white Cheltenham Town pizza in the shape of a Robins shirt!

Cheltenham resembled a ghost town as thousands of Robins fans left to make their way to Cardiff. On the first day of sales, a record 7,000 tickets were sold, eclipsing the 5,500 the club sold on the first day of business before the FA Trophy final at Wembley four years earlier. Superb support made the Welsh national stadium feel like home for the day. Two of the key figures in the club's meteoric rise, Chris Banks and Lee Howells, were ruled out through injury, but with more than 17,000 fans cheering them on, Cheltenham took the lead after twenty-seven minutes. Martin Devaney, who had not been a regular in the side, repaid the faith shown in him by his manager by producing a man-of-the-match performance on the left wing and it was the Cheltenham-born player who opened the scoring. Devaney bamboozled Diamonds' left-back Tarkan Mustafa and tore into the penalty area. He then took the ball past Mark Peters and played a one-two with Rushden's Garry Butterworth before beating Billy Turley from an acute angle. He celebrated by ripping his shirt off and running to the empty side of the stadium, but he was not alone for long and it was only a few seconds before he was caught up and mobbed by his jubilant team mates.

Cheltenham were then guilty of a lapse in concentration as they seemed to still be celebrating the opening goal when Jamaican international Paul Hall ran straight through the middle and beat Steve Book, almost unchallenged. Striker Onandi Lowe looked dangerous in attack for Brian Talbot's side and Book had to be on top form to keep the scores level at the break. If the first half was a relatively even display, Cheltenham raised their game in the second period and took almost complete control of the match. Top scorer Julian Alsop was proving to be a handful against his old Bristol Rovers team mate Andy Tillson and Alsop hit his twenty-sixth goal of the season shortly after the interval. Lee Williams and Antony Griffin linked up on the right and Alsop nodded down a deep cross to Tony Naylor. Naylor was challenged by Tillson, but the ball broke to Alsop who made no mistake from close range. At half-time Cotterill had advised his players not to go over the top with any possible goal celebrations in light of what happened after Devaney's strike, but Supporters' Player of the Year Alsop was determined to savour the moment.

John Finnigan curls in Cheltenham's third goal to put the seal on the Robins' promotion to League One.

Veteran Neil Grayson, instrumental in the Robins' promotion from the Conference three years earlier, was given his chance to help them make another step up the footballing ladder coming off the bench after seventy-five minutes. It did not take long for Grayson to make an impact in what was to be his last game for the club. Williams' pass found the Yorkshireman on the left and his rasping drive rattled the bar and rebounded to John Finnigan, who composed himself and curled a well-placed shot around Turley to make the game safe after eighty minutes. Finnigan was celebrating one of the highlights of his career only two months after arriving from cash-strapped Lincoln City on a free transfer as a replacement for the injured Howells, who broke his leg in a win at Bristol Rovers.

Steve Cotterill after his last match as manager of Cheltenham.

The Robins are able to toast promotion to the third tier of English football for the first time.

After a long, hard season that started slowly, but produced a record-breaking FA Cup run to the last sixteen, Cheltenham had made it to what is now League One. It was hard to take in for many fans, who could look forward to visiting clubs such as Swindon Town and Bristol City when five years earlier they were travelling to Baldock Town and Ashford Town. It was another memorable occasion for the Robins, and Rushden boss Talbot showed great sportsmanship after the match, visiting the Cheltenham dressing room to congratulate the team on what was a thoroughly deserved victory. The masterful Cotterill said after the game that his team had done it the hard way, but also the best way. Cheltenham paraded around the town in an open-top bus to celebrate their third and final promotion under his leadership. Fans called for the borough council to make Cotterill a freeman of the borough – the highest honour it can bestow. The all-conquering manager was in demand and despite interest from Harry Redknapp's Portsmouth and Wimbledon, he left to join Stoke City for a brief spell as boss before moving on to top-flight club Sunderland, where he worked as number two to Howard Wilkinson.

Cheltenham's wonderful travelling support at Cardiff.

Cheltenham Town: Book, Griffin, Victory, Duff, Walker, Williams, Yates, Finnigan, Devaney (Grayson 75), Naylor, Alsop. Subs not used: Howarth, Muggleton, Lee, Tyson.
Rushden & Diamonds: Turley, Mustafa, Underwood, Peters, Tillson, Gray (Brady 69), Wardley, Butterworth, Hall, Lowe, Partridge (Angell 69). Subs not used: Pennock, Setchell, Hunter.
Referee: Mr A.R. Leake.
Attendance: 24,368.

MATCH 38: NORWICH CITY V. CHELTENHAM TOWN

Worthington Cup First Round
Tuesday 10 September 2002, Carrow Road
Norwich City 0
Cheltenham Town 3 (Naylor 30, 45, McAuley 83)

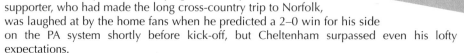

Graham Allner lasted for only thirty-two games in the Cheltenham Town managerial hot seat, but this was a memorable night for the club and undoubtedly the finest moment of Allner's brief tenure. Cheltenham had narrowly lost to the Canaries over two legs in the same competition three years earlier, but they embarrassed their Championship opponents with a stunning performance in this one-legged tie. Boss Nigel Worthington's Norwich side were lying in third place in the race for promotion to the Premiership, and League One outfit Cheltenham were without a win in their seven matches since the play-off victory over Rushden & Diamonds at the end of the previous campaign. One optimistic Robins supporter, who had made the long cross-country trip to Norfolk, was laughed at by the home fans when he predicted a 2–0 win for his side on the PA system shortly before kick-off, but Cheltenham surpassed even his lofty expectations.

Allner made one change to the side that had drawn 1–1 at Colchester United in the league three days earlier, replacing Paul Brayson with John Finnigan. Finnigan made the most of his return to a non-stop effort in midfield, while central defenders Michael Duff and Richard Walker handled Iwan Roberts well. Wales international striker Roberts scored twice in the first leg of the 1999 tie between the two sides, won 3–2 by the Canaries on aggregate.

David Nielsen, in the side ahead of leading scorer Paul McVeigh, missed early chances for Norwich, who were winners of the competition in 1962 and 1985 and runners-up in 1973 and 1975. The Canaries had lost 3–2 to Sheffield United the previous weekend, ending a thirteen-match unbeaten run at Carrow Road. Two first-half goals from Tony Naylor then silenced the majority of the disbelieving Carrow Road crowd. Naylor's first, his third of the season, came on the half hour after a defensive header intended for his goalkeeper by Malky Mackay. Naylor stole in ahead of the now England international goalkeeper Robert Green, and unleashed a well-struck shot into the net from a tight angle. Roberts went close to equalising with a powerful header, but Naylor doubled the Robins' lead on the stroke of half-time, drilling home from the edge of the area after a slide rule pass from the excellent Duff.

Norwich included defender Darren Kenton in their line-up, who went on to play fifteen times for Cheltenham during the 2008/09 campaign. They were booed off by their fans at the break, but they started the second half more purposefully as they looked to battle their way back into the tie. Roberts again threatened, but Steve Book's handling was flawless and the Cheltenham number one also denied Alex Notman and the Robins survived a scramble when Gary Holt dispossessed Walker.

Dane Steen Nedergaard volleyed beyond the far post as Norwich became more urgent and Hugh McAuley shot powerfully past a post in the eightieth minute. It was McAuley who sealed the biggest upset of the round with eight minutes remaining. The midfielder, who was released by outgoing boss Steve Cotterill and subsequently re-signed by Allner, curled home a delightful shot after Russell Milton had touched a free-kick to him inside the area. The free-kick had been awarded after Green contrived to pick up a back-pass from Mackay when the whole of Carrow Road expected him to clear with his feet. Norwich, three down with seven minutes to play and two added on, never looked like getting back into the tie and Cheltenham progressed to round two with a degree of comfort. The Robins were given a much-deserved standing ovation from the entire ground and even Norwich director Delia Smith clapped and waved to the Cheltenham fans as they left the ground.

'How's that?' Tony Naylor after netting at Carrow Road to leave Norwich stunned.

Allner was understandably delighted with his side's performance and hoped the game would mark a turnaround in league form. He said:

> We did it on merit and Norwich were very kind in their comments afterwards. Their first-team coach, Doug Livermore, said we'd deserved it and we've threatened to do this in the other matches we've played. We took our chances, we've kept a clean sheet and it wasn't a fluke result. It was a fair reflection of the way the game went. They didn't overly threaten us and we kept the ball well at times. We set out to try to frustrate them by keeping as much possession as we could. The defence played very, very well, the midfield worked extremely hard and the front men produced. It was totally a team effort.

Worthington accused his players of showing Cheltenham disrespect and demanded an immediate improvement as the Canaries were about to take on their arch enemies Ipswich the following Sunday. They drew 1–1 at Portman Road and went on to finish eighth in the table.

Cheltenham had fallen at the first hurdle in their previous three League Cup campaigns. After their superb win over Norwich, they were drawn to play Crystal Palace away in round two, when they suffered their heaviest defeat as a Football League club, going down 7–0 at Selhurst Park. Former Kidderminster Harriers boss Allner lost his job in January 2003, replaced by Bobby Gould, who failed to save Cheltenham from an immediate return to the basement division after a final day defeat at Notts County.

Norwich City: Green, Nedergaard, Kenton, Mackay, Drury, Notman, Mulryne (Emblen 87), Holt, Easton (Heckingbottom 62), Roberts, Nielsen (Llewellyn 70). Subs not used: Crichton, Russell.
Cheltenham Town: Book, Howarth, Walker, Duff, Victory, McAuley, Finnigan, Yates, Milton, Alsop, Naylor. Subs not used: Higgs, Brough, Brayson, Devaney, Williams.
Referee: G. Hegley (Herts).
Attendance: 13,285.

Match 39: Cheltenham Town v. Northampton Town

Nationwide League Division Three
Friday 5 September 2003, Whaddon Road
Cheltenham Town 4 (Taylor 56,
  Forsyth 76 pen, 90 pen, Devaney 90)
Northampton Town 3 (Dudfield 24, 32,
  Smith 73 pen)

Substitute Richard Forsyth kept his head to convert two late penalties, one of which was a retake, and Martin Devaney snatched a ninety-second-minute winner to sink Northampton Town in a thrilling Friday night goal feast. Manager Bobby Gould had labelled his side 'the entertainers' and on this evidence it was easy to see why. They had already drawn 3–3 at Hull City and lost 4–3 to Swansea City in the opening month of the campaign and the goals continued to flow at Whaddon Road.

Cheltenham fought back from 2–0 down and 3–1 down with the aid of a top-quality goal by Bob Taylor and two penalties by midfielder Forsyth. The second Forsyth penalty was in the ninetieth minute, making it 3–3 before Devaney snatched a dramatic clincher in the second minute of additional time. The only frustration on a night of great entertainment was the performance of referee Trevor Kettle, who infuriated fans and players of both teams with some highly questionable decisions. Kettle cautioned three players from each side and allowed a controversial first goal for Northampton to stand. The Cheltenham fans fumed after goalkeeper Shane Higgs had gone up with a clutch of Cobblers players for a twenty-third-minute cross by midfielder Paul Harsley. Higgs got both hands to the ball but it dropped to the ground and Lawrie Dudfield was accredited with the last touch during the scramble. The Cheltenham supporters behind the goal at the Prestbury Road end felt that Higgs had been impeded, but referee Kettle was having none of it and two minutes later he irritated them again by booking Kayode Odejayi for a foul when trying to retrieve the ball in the Northampton box.

Frenchman Bertrand Cozic had already been cautioned and it got worse for Cheltenham when a mistake by Michael Duff ended with Dudfield breaking away for Northampton's second in the thirty-second minute. Duff had decided to make one of his charges up field, but he lost the ball to substitute Oliver Burgess as he approached the halfway line. Burgess's stabbed pass through the middle left Dudfield with a clear run on goal and although Higgs got a touch, his low shot nestled in a corner. Until that stage, a Northampton team that included Josh Low, who went on to join the Robins in 2008, had commanded the game and Cheltenham did not have an effort on target until just before half-time. Then, Jamie Victory got up to head a corner down towards the goal line, but goalkeeper Glyn Thompson dropped on it.

Gould told his team at half-time that he wanted them to deliver twenty-two crosses in forty-five minutes. He got seventeen and it was enough to turn the match on its head. The Cheltenham fight-back began with the kind of goal they were expecting from veteran Taylor. He had his back to goal when he moved onto a nodded pass by Cozic, pushed the ball to his right and turned and drove it into Thompson's top left corner ten minutes into the second half. A minute later Taylor was being cautioned for arguing with referee Kettle after being penalised for a challenge on Thompson. Two minutes later, Odejayi threw himself at Garham Fyfe's cross and headed it wide from six yards.

Cheltenham had to survive another blow after seventy-two minutes when Cozic chased after Martin Smith who hit the ground when challenged in the penalty area and stood up to score from the spot-kick. At that stage, Cozic and Antony Griffin were taken off and Forsyth and Lee Howells

Richard Forsyth held his nerve.

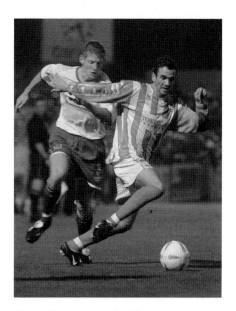

Martin Devaney snatched the winner.

were sent on. Griffin was playing because Kevin Amankwaah strained an Achilles tendon in his front room on Thursday night.

Three minutes after Northampton's penalty, Cheltenham were awarded one for a push by Ian Sampson on Taylor. Forsyth, who was to have a profound effect on the game, slammed it along the ground into Thompson's right corner. Forsyth had not started a Division Three match since damaging his back the previous January and it was his first touch of the game. There followed another substitution with Odejayi going off and Paul Brayson going on in time to witness the pulsating finish. In the last minute of normal time, Victory took a return pass from Brayson and Burgess tripped him in the box. Forsyth put the penalty into exactly the same spot he had put the last. It did not end there. Referee Kettle decided there had been an encroachment into the penalty area and ordered the kick to be retaken, so Forsyth, admirably cool, hit the same spot again. A point would probably have been enough for Cheltenham in the circumstances, but Devaney made it three when the ball skimmed off the heads of Sampson and Reid and left him clear to beat Thompson. After the game the remarkably calm Forsyth said he would step aside and allow regular penalty-taker Grant McCann, away with Northern Ireland at the time, to resume his penalty duties the next time Cheltenham were awarded a spot kick. Forsyth was the regular penalty-taker at Kidderminster Harriers before he moved into the Football League with Birmingham City in 1995. In a similar match for Harriers against Yeovil Town in 1989, he scored one, hit a post with a second and scored the third in the final minute to set up a 3–2 win.

After this victory, ex-Wimbledon, Cardiff City and Wales international boss Gould only managed to oversee one more win out of nine as manager before he resigned dramatically after a 2–0 home defeat by Rochdale on 18 October.

Cheltenham Town: Higgs, Griffin (Howells 74), Jones, M. Duff, Victory, Devaney, Cozic (Forsyth 74), Yates, Fyfe, Taylor, Odejayi (Brayson 81). Subs not used: Book, Cleverley.
Northampton Town: Thompson, Chambers, Sampson, Reid, Clark (Carruthers 85), Low, Westwood (Burgess 21), Harsley, Hargreaves, Dudfield, Smith (Richards 81). Subs not used: Youngs, Harper.
Referee: T. Kettle.
Attendance: 5,002.

MATCH 40: CHELTENHAM TOWN V. LINCOLN CITY

Nationwide League Division Three
Saturday 6 March 2004, Whaddon Road
Cheltenham Town 3 (McCann 32, Finnigan 87,
 Odejayi 90)
Lincoln City 2 (Richardson 3, 45 pen)

Manager John Ward's Cheltenham Town snatched victory from the jaws of defeat in an enthralling contest at Whaddon Road during the 2003/04 season. Ward is something of a Lincoln City legend, having made over 200 appearances for the Imps between 1971 and 1982, but there was no room for sentimentality with three valuable Division Three points at stake.

Marcus Richardson gave the Imps an early lead, latching onto a through ball and slotting the ball past goalkeeper Shane Higgs with three minutes gone. After their setback, Cheltenham battled their way back into the game and Paul Brayson came close to netting an equaliser. After a period of sustained pressure, Grant McCann levelled the scores with a well-struck free-kick. There had been appeals for a penalty after Richard Liburd handled a Martin Devaney cross, but the referee adjudged the offence to have taken place outside the area. McCann fired home from the edge of the box after thirty-two minutes and Liburd was cautioned for his deliberate handball. Three minutes before half time Liburd was given a second yellow card and his marching orders after a foul on Cheltenham right-back Antony Griffin. Ten-man Lincoln rallied and scored on the stroke of half time. It was Richardson again, this time from the penalty spot. The big striker had been brought down by Michael Duff and he stepped up to send Higgs the wrong way and restore his side's advantage.

John Finnigan levelled against his old club before Kayode Odejayi won it for Cheltenham.

Damian Spencer uses his strength.

The second half was dominated by Cheltenham, but stubborn defence from Lincoln frustrated the Robins and as the final whistle approached, it appeared as though Keith Alexander's men had done enough to claim the win. Ward introduced Kayode Odejayi in place of Brayson and the Nigerian began to cause problems immediately with his height and pace. John Brough came close with a powerful shot on the turn and Damian Spencer blazed over the bar after taking advantage of some loose defensive play. The breakthrough finally arrived with three minutes remaining, and it was former Lincoln skipper John Finnigan who broke the hearts of the travelling fans. Devaney's corner was half-cleared and the ball fell to the midfield dynamo, who struck the ball on the half-volley past the despairing dive of Alan Marriott. Finnigan had left Lincoln to join Cheltenham two years earlier. It looked as though a point had been saved, but deep into injury time, Odejayi leapt highest to head home a Devaney cross and seal an unlikely, but thrilling win for Ward's improving team, who went on to finish fourteenth that season.

Cheltenham Town: Higgs, Griffin (Gill 71), M. Duff, Brough, Victory, Devaney, Finnigan, Forsyth (Cleverley 65), McCann, Spencer, Brayson (Odejayi 78). Subs not used: Book, Bird.
Lincoln City: Marriott, Weaver, Morgan, Bloomer, Wattley, Sedgemore, Gain, Liburd, Green (Pearce 87), Richardson (Cropper 70), Yeo. Subs not used: May, Gordon, Trout.
Referee: L.E. Cable (Surrey).
Attendance: 3,783.

Match 41: Cheltenham Town v. Newcastle United

FA Cup Fourth Round
Saturday 28 January 2006, Whaddon Road
Cheltenham Town 0
Newcastle United 2 (Chopra 41, Parker 43)

John Ward's Cheltenham Town were thrown into the national spotlight as Newcastle United came to town for an FA Cup glamour tie in January 2006. It was the first time a top flight club had played a competitive match at Whaddon Road and the fourth-round clash was televised live by the BBC.

The Robins did themselves and their town proud, matching their illustrious opponents and outplaying them for long periods, but two messy goals separated the two sides at the final whistle. Cheltenham had reached the fourth round for only the second time in their history with wins over Carlisle United, Oxford United and Chester City. They had needed replays to oust Oxford and Chester, meaning that the Newcastle test was their sixth FA Cup match of the season. The Magpies, six times winners of the competition, had beaten Mansfield

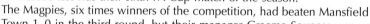

Town 1–0 in the third round, but their manager Graeme Souness was under fire due to poor Premier League form and many onlookers sensed an upset could be on the cards. The nation watched with interest as Alan Shearer aimed to break Jackie Milburn's record and become Newcastle's all-time leading goalscorer. It was also a chance for some of Cheltenham's leading lights to put themselves in the shop window, with Kayode Odejayi and Brian Wilson in particular generating interest from higher division clubs.

Robins midfielder David Bird went into the game knowing that his wife Nikki was due to give birth to their first child. Bird, who had a poster of Shearer on his bedroom wall when he was a youngster, started in place of the injured Grant McCann alongside skipper John Finnigan, but it was Nikki who stole most of the limelight sat in the stand.

After all the hype, kick-off finally arrived at 12.30 p.m. on a bitterly cold January afternoon, but the atmosphere inside the packed ground was red hot. Groundsman Mike Heather's pitch was praised by BBC co-commentator Mark Lawrenson, who said it was 'worthy of a Premier League club.' Newcastle looked beatable and fragile despite their host of international stars and Cheltenham, led by the inspirational Finnigan, took the game to the Geordies. Young central defenders Michael Townsend and Gavin Caines ensured that Shearer hardly had a kick and at no stage did he look likely to net a landmark 201st goal for his beloved Magpies. Odejayi had the game's first real chance in the twelfth minute, sending the ball wide after frightening Newcastle with his electric pace, but it looked as though Cheltenham had reached half time on level terms. However, Newcastle took a barely deserved lead in the forty-first minute. With Finnigan controlling the middle of the pitch, Cheltenham were having the better of the play, but Celestine Babayaro raced onto a headed pass from Nolberto Solano and as Shane Higgs threw himself at the Nigerian's feet, the ball spun off him and dropped towards the goal, but Chopra jumped above Townsend and headed in. Newcastle, wearing an all-blue change strip had Scott Parker back in midfield after a cartilage operation and he knew nothing about the second goal that deflated Whaddon Road only two minutes after Chopra's opener. Jerry Gill kicked away Peter Ramage's cross from the right and it hit the unknowing Parker and bounced past Higgs.

Cheltenham refused to lie down despite the double blow and they started the second half strongly. Shay Given took a cross from JJ Melligan off Steve Guinan's head and Guinan made a chance himself with a turn past the hapless Jean-Alain Boumsoung and a shot from the right corner of the box which flew past Given's post. Boumsong was given a torrid time by Odejayi throughout and he

Man-of-the-match John Finnigan closes down Alan Shearer in front of a packed Whaddon Road crowd.

Kayode Odejayi was a thorn in Newcastle's side all afternoon.

survived shouts for a penalty when the Robins striker ended in a heap in the fifty-fourth minute. Odejayi, who was in demand, with the likes of Stoke City, Leicester City, Plymouth Argyle, Millwall and Coventry City all watching him, had his big moment in the seventy-sixth minute. It was Odejayi whose goal took Cheltenham through their high-pressure third-round replay at Chester, but when Craig Armstrong played him through the middle he took it around Given expertly before sending his shot wide, later claiming the ball had bobbled as he struck it.

Newcastle then had enough quality and composure to keep the ball with multi-pass moves, running down the clock as Cheltenham were left to rue missed opportunities that could have earned them a money-spinning replay at St James' Park. They still netted a substantial six-figure sum from their big day and the brave cup run was the catalyst for an excellent second half of the season that saw them win promotion from Coca-Cola League Two via the play-offs. The cup funds also allowed Ward to sign loan striker Steven Gillespie from Bristol City permanently for a nominal fee and less than three years later he was sold to Colchester United for a deal that could rise in excess of £400,000.

Robins youth team player Emre Woolf, whose mother is Turkish, met one his heroes Emre Belozoglu after the game and left the ground proudly clutching the Turkey international star's match shirt. Shearer's shirt ended up in the possession of a delighted nineteen-year-old Townsend.

Cheltenham Town: Higgs, Gill, Caines, Townsend, Armstrong, Melligan (Vincent 85), Finnigan, Bird, Wilson, Odejayi, Guinan (Spencer 74). Subs not used: Duff, Connolly, Brown.
Newcastle United: Given, Ramage, Bramble, Boumsong, Babayaro, Solano (Emre 58), Clark, Parker (Luque 75), Ameobi, Shearer, Chopra (N'Zogbia 65). Subs not used: Elliott, Harper.
Referee: M. Riley (West Yorkshire).
Attendance: 7,022.

Match 42: Mansfield v. Cheltenham Town

Coca-Cola League Two
Saturday 6 May 2006, Field Mill
Mansfield Town 0
Cheltenham Town 5 (Gillespie 34, Vincent 45,
McCann 50, Bird 81 pen, Odejayi 85)

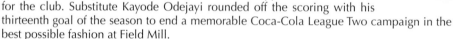

Cheltenham Town turned on the style to record their biggest win as a Football League club on the final day of the 2005/06 regular season and put themselves in a perfect frame of mind for their imminent play-off challenge. Boss John Ward made five changes to the team that defeated Notts County 2–0 seven days earlier to seal a play-off place, but first-half goals from the returning Steven Gillespie and Ashley Vincent opened the floodgates and shell-shocked Mansfield caved in during the second period. Grant McCann scored a goal that was from the top drawer even by his own high standards, and David Bird safely despatched a penalty to register his first goal for Cheltenham on his 127th appearance for the club. Substitute Kayode Odejayi rounded off the scoring with his thirteenth goal of the season to end a memorable Coca-Cola League Two campaign in the best possible fashion at Field Mill.

Young right-back Andy Gallinagh was handed his first start for the club and the twenty-one-year-old took the step up to senior football in his stride, recovering from a nervy opening to give an encouraging account of himself. Regular right-back Jerry Gill was one of four players rested. Craig Armstrong was also missing from the match day squad with an injury, so Mickey Bell played at left-back. Captain John Finnigan was given the day off and Bird deputised alongside stand-in skipper McCann. Gillespie made his first appearance since 11 March, having recovered from a hamstring tear and the striker looked sharp and bright enough to force himself into contention for the play-off semi-final first-leg clash at Wycombe. Vincent, who scored his first goal of the season after going on as a substitute a week earlier, replaced JJ Melligan on the right of midfield.

Three weeks before Ward took the managerial reins, Cheltenham were beaten 4–0 at Mansfield. Only three of the players who played that day started this game – Shane Higgs, David Bird and Grant McCann. It is a measure of how much restructuring had been carried out since November 2003 and how much the team had changed. Despite the unfamiliar line-up, Cheltenham produced some slick football early on, but the noisy travelling fans in the away stand had to wait until thirty-four minutes for the opening goal. Bird showed good technique to play a controlled pass on the volley to Steve Guinan on the right. Guinan played a return pass to Bird, who threaded the ball through to Gillespie and in a flash the twenty-year-old had half-turned his marker and placed a measured shot into Stags goalkeeper Jason White's bottom right post. It all happened so quickly apart from the finish, which rolled almost in slow motion into the net, but its accuracy put it beyond White's reach. In the final minute of the first half, Vincent scored his second goal in two weeks. He latched on to a misplaced defensive pass from Stephen Dawson just inside the Mansfield half, travelled at pace into the penalty area and applied a confident finish past White.

Cheltenham picked up where they had left off after the break and McCann exchanged passes with Vincent from a short corner on the right and, unopposed, curled a measured shot into the top right corner, prompting even large sections of the home support to applaud generously. Gillespie was withdrawn after an hour, with Damian Spencer going on to make his fifty-eighth appearance of the season and continue his record of featuring in every match that season. Adam Connolly went on in place of McCann, with Shane Duff taking the captain's armband and Odejayi replaced Guinan. With ten minutes left, Brian Wilson's corner was headed towards goal by Gavin Caines. Defender Rhys Day used his arm to block Caines' effort and the referee awarded a penalty. Caines initially

Ashley Vincent's performance earned him a place in Cheltenham's team for their play-off challenge.

placed the ball on the spot, but – with some encouragement from the travelling hordes – Bird was given the chance to open his account. The twenty-one-year-old, who scored a hat-trick for Cinderford Town as a fifteen-year-old, calmly sent White the wrong way and was instantly mobbed by his team-mates as the drought was put to an end. Odejayi shot over the bar after Vincent had threaded a ball through, but the Nigerian-born striker made no mistake with another chance. Spencer provided the pass and Odejayi beat White, who may feel he should have done better. Wilson was denied by the legs of White in the closing minutes, but it was Cheltenham's day and Wycombe would not have been looking forward to playing a team in that sort of rampant form.

Ward described Cheltenham's performance at Mansfield as 'something special' as the Robins ran riot to record their biggest Football League win. The 5–0 win at Field Mill ensured that Cheltenham finished fifth in Coca-Cola League Two and they would take on sixth-placed Wycombe in the play-off semi-finals, with the first leg in Buckinghamshire. It was Cheltenham's biggest victory in any league match since November 1996, when they beat Ashford Town 6–0 at Whaddon Road in the Southern League Premier Division. 'It was one of those days when you just say "wow, that was a little bit special and a little bit different,"' Ward said. 'It couldn't have gone any better and we have been as clinical as we have ever been and shared the scoring round, so it was a fantastic effort from everyone. I wanted to win and finish with seventy-two points and I am very pleased to say everything we tried came off.'

Cheltenham Town: Higgs, Gallinagh, Caines, Duff, Bell, Vincent, Bird, McCann (Connolly 65), Wilson, Guinan, (Odejayi 74) Gillespie (Spencer 60). Subs not used: Brown, Wylde.
Mansfield Town: White, Jacobs, Day, Baptiste, Wilson, Birchall (Uhlenbeek 68), D'Laryea, Dawson (Rundle 58), Lloyd, Barker, Arnold (Russell 58). Subs not used: Pressman, Coke.
Referee: K. Hill (Hertfordshire).
Attendance: 3,728.

Match 43: Wycombe Wanderers v. Cheltenham Town

Coca-Cola League Two play-off semi-final, first leg
Saturday 13 May 2006, Adams Park
Wycombe Wanderers 1 (Mooney 90)
Cheltenham Town 2 (Finnigan 43, Guinan 75)

Cheltenham Town travelled to old non-league adversaries Wycombe Wanderers for the first leg of their Coca-Cola League Two play-off semi-final. They raced into a two-goal lead, before Tommy Mooney handed Wycombe a ninetieth-minute lifeline at the Causeway Stadium. The former Cheltenham transfer target's last-gasp strike left the tie delicately balanced ahead of the second leg at Whaddon Road five days later, and took the gloss off what was an accomplished performance from John Ward's Robins.

Before Mooney's goal boosted Wycombe's hopes, a resilient defensive performance and excellent goals from John Finnigan and Steve Guinan had put Cheltenham in a strong position. Wycombe made a blistering start as they had done in the league meeting between the two sides in March, but Cheltenham's defence held firm with Shane Duff outstanding. Both sets of supporters created a fantastic atmosphere as the contest started fifteen minutes later than scheduled due to the late finish of the FA Cup final. Ward made four changes to the team that defeated Mansfield Town seven days earlier, with Jerry Gill, Craig Armstrong, John Finnigan and Kayode Odejayi replacing Andy Gallinagh, Mickey Bell, David Bird and Steven Gillespie in the starting line-up. JJ Melligan, who had been rested at Mansfield, did not return after a chicken pox scare, so Ashley Vincent continued on the right of midfield.

Wycombe controlled the opening twenty-five minutes, with Cheltenham forced to defend in numbers and break at speed. The first chance arrived after twelve minutes when Gavin Caines allowed a high ball to bounce and Mooney ghosted in at the far post. The ex-Birmingham City and Watford man fired the ball across to Russell Martin, but Duff made a brave block. A similar Mooney cross from the left two minutes later hit Duff and ricocheted over the bar off Wycombe defender Will Antwi. Craig Armstrong had his work cut out dealing with Wycombe's right flank of Danny Senda and Kevin Betsy, but the gritty left-back nullified the highly-rated duo's threat with the help of Brian Wilson. Wycombe lost Rob Lee to a facial injury sustained in an aerial challenge with Guinan after twenty-nine minutes. The forty-year-old former England international left the field with blood pouring from his face and needed eight stitches around his eye. It was another eight minutes before Wycombe gave up hope of Lee rejoining the action and he was replaced by Joe Burnell. Guinan, who received a yellow card for the challenge, was adamant that there was no intent and apologised to Lee immediately after being substituted in the second half.

Odejayi threatened for the first time while Wycombe were down to ten men, racing on to a huge clearance from Higgs and challenging goalkeeper Steve Williams, but Roger Johnson cleared the danger. Duff made another crucial headed clearance after Martin had connected with Senda's free-kick and for all Wycombe's possession, Shane Higgs' only action was dealing with some testing crosses from both wings. Cheltenham's first notable attempt on goal arrived four minutes before half time when Odejayi forced a save from Williams, who was making only his third start of the season. Guinan fired in another shot on target a minute later and with the pattern of the game changing, Cheltenham took the lead after forty-three minutes. Guinan was fouled by Senda and McCann's free-kick was pumped deep into the Wycombe penalty area, where Duff was waiting. The defender had won every header at the back and he beat Clint Easton and nodded the ball down. Finnigan was quick to react and after holding off Matt Bloomfield's challenge, the Robins skipper sent a well-placed low shot through Burnell's legs and inside the far post.

Duff made yet another superb block from Mooney's header early in the second half as Wycombe started brightly again. Acting manager Steve Brown sent on Jermaine Easter in place of Ian Stonebridge in an attempt to unsettle the Cheltenham defence, but an unmarked Guinan went close to extending Cheltenham's lead from McCann's free-kick, though he steered his header wide. The accuracy of McCann's deliveries were causing Wycombe major problems and, after a short pass from Gill, McCann found Duff, who should have scored with a diving header, but he failed to make a significant contact. Easter's first-time effort on the turn drifted wide with

A delighted John Finnigan opened the scoring.

Higgs at full stretch and substitute Stefan Oakes went close with a curling free-kick.

Cheltenham doubled their lead with easily the best move of the match after seventy-five minutes. Vincent initiated the attack with a diagonal run before Wilson and McCann combined to find Guinan. He exchanged passes with Odejayi, continuing his run into the area and beating Williams at his near post with a well-struck drive that deflected off Johnson's arm. Cheltenham had one foot in the Millennium Stadium final, but Wycombe staged a late rally in a bid to reduce the arrears. Armstrong was adjudged to have impeded Mooney and Martin's deep free-kick was kept in play by Antwi and sent back into the middle where Mooney arrived to smash an unstoppable shot past Higgs and set up a mouthwatering second leg.

A tremendous defensive display booked Cheltenham's place in the play-off final against Grimsby Town at the Millennium Stadium. Wycombe enjoyed superior possession for much of the contest, but Cheltenham defended as though their lives depended on it and shut them out. For all Wycombe's territorial dominance, Higgs was rarely called into action, largely thanks to his back four. Duff and Caines in particular were impenetrable at the heart of the Robins defence. Wycombe's hero of the first leg, Mooney, went close in the first half, but he was largely restricted to half chances. Wanderers lost Mooney during the second half and with their leading scorer's departure went his side's promotion hopes. Guinan missed a chance for Cheltenham, hitting Vincent's cross over the bar, but it didn't matter. Over the two legs of the semi-final, Wycombe showed what a fine footballing side they were, but the second leg was all about heart and Cheltenham showed it in abundance to reach their second play-off final. There were jubilant scenes at Whaddon Road when the final whistle blew and a collective sigh of relief was followed by celebrations that went on long into the night.

Wycombe Wanderers: Williams, Senda, Johnson, Antwi, Easton, Betsy, Bloomfield (Oakes 63), Lee (Burnell 37), Martin, Stonebridge (Easter 54) Mooney. Subs not used: Talia, Williamson.
Cheltenham Town: Higgs, Gill, Duff, Caines, Armstrong, Vincent, Finnigan, McCann, Wilson (Bell 82), Guinan (Gillespie 80), Odejayi (Spencer 80). Subs not used: Brown, Bird.
Referee: A. Hall (West Midlands).
Attendance: 5,936.

MATCH 44: CHELTENHAM TOWN V. GRIMSBY TOWN

Coca-Cola League Two play-off final
Sunday 28 May 2006, Millennium Stadium
Cheltenham Town 1 (Guinan 63)
Grimsby Town 0

Steve Guinan was the hero as Cheltenham Town rounded off a memorable season in the best possible style at the Millennium Stadium to earn promotion to League One for the second time in four years. In what could have been his last match for the club, out-of-contract striker Guinan struck after sixty-three minutes to sink Grimsby and earn Cheltenham promotion back into the third tier of English football.

Grant McCann saw his second-half penalty saved by Grimsby goalkeeper Steve Mildenhall, but it was irrelevant. Cheltenham's second play-off triumph sent them into dreamland and back up to League One after a three-year absence. The largest crowd ever to witness a Robins match gathered in Cardiff's impressive arena for what was the last play-off final to be held in the Welsh capital.

Robins boss John Ward handed a surprise recall to Steven Gillespie, who replaced leading scorer Kayode Odejayi and partnered Guinan in attack. A fired-up Cheltenham took the initiative from kick-off and both Gillespie and Guinan missed opportunities early on. Gillespie, who was on the bench for both legs of the semi-final victory over Wycombe, raced onto a through-ball from McCann and nudged himself goalside of Rob Jones after eight minutes. Faced with Mildenhall, Gillespie's second touch was heavy and allowed Mildenhall to spread himself and deflect the ball for a corner.

Nerves appeared to be getting the better of Grimsby and three minutes later Guinan was gifted the ball from Rob Jones' weak back header. The striker had more time and space than he thought and his hurried effort was comfortably held by the Mariners' number one.

Shane Duff was part of a tremendous defensive effort to keep Grimsby out.

Steve Guinan and Kayode Odejayi.

Grimsby's first attempt on goal arrived after twelve minutes, with Curtis Woodhouse's wayward shot drifting high over the bar, but Cheltenham were the better side. Guinan received a pass from Craig Armstrong and shot wide of the left upright, but Armstrong's final came to an abrupt end after twenty-four minutes. He leapt with Michael Reddy to nod a huge clearance from Mildenhall back to his goalkeeper Shane Higgs, but the two players clashed heads and ended up in a heap on the floor. Armstrong broke his nose in the collision and left the field immediately for treatment. He did not reappear and was replaced by thirty-four-year-old Mickey Bell, who took up the left-back berth and made his twelfth appearance for the club. Reddy was out cold immediately after the clash and was also unfit to continue. The striker was replaced by the speedy Gary Cohen, who joined Gary Jones up front. Bell's first contribution was a well-struck drive that was deflected for a corner. Woodhouse, who was playing his final match before embarking on a professional boxing career, floated in a free-kick that was safely claimed by Higgs, but Grimsby improved steadily as the half wore on. A strong run from Cohen was ended by a well-timed tackle from Jerry Gill, and Paul Bolland fed Andy Parkinson, who dodged the challenge of Gavin Caines and fell to the ground looking for a penalty. The referee waved away his protests. John Finnigan needed treatment after receiving a bang on the face from Cohen, but the Robins skipper battled on.

Grimsby finished the half on top and Parkinson found Cohen, who ran away from Caines and tried his luck with a low shot that Higgs did well to parry low to his right. Parkinson and Bolland both shot over as the opening period ended goalless.

Caines headed a McCann corner at Mildenhall with the first action of the second half, and McCann was given a ticking off by the referee for a foul on Woodhouse. Surprise starter Gillespie sustained an injury after a challenge with the giant figure of Rob Jones and Odejayi was sent on in the twenty-year-old's place after sixty-two minutes. Barely a minute later there were scenes of wild celebration in the Cheltenham end of the stadium as the deadlock was broken. Guinan received a poor clearance on the right of the penalty area, cut inside and sent over a low cross to the far post with his left foot. The curling delivery evaded Ashley Vincent and Odejayi, but the Cheltenham pair did enough to distract Mildenhall and the ball crept into the bottom right corner of his goal.

John Ward hoists aloft the League Two play-off trophy.

Cheltenham were handed a golden opportunity to double their lead seven minutes later. Woodhouse was dispossessed in the centre circle and McCann led the charge back into the Grimsby half. The Northern Ireland international exchanged passes with Odejayi and found himself through on goal. He took the ball around the advancing Mildenhall and, as he shaped to roll the ball into the empty net, he was sent crashing to the ground by Woodhouse. Woodhouse inconceivably escaped further punishment and McCann's spot-kick was saved by Mildenhall to restore hope for Russell Slade's men. The frantic action continued and McCann came desperately close to making up for his penalty miss, clipping a delicate shot against the bar, with Mildenhall well beaten. The rebound fell to Brian Wilson, who looked certain to score at the far post, but Mildenhall scampered across his goal and kept the ball out. Slade sent on towering central defender Ben Futcher up front in a bid to salvage a goal in the last fifteen minutes. For Cheltenham, Damian Spencer replaced Vincent on the right to make his sixty-first appearance of the season. Higgs made the most important save of his career with ten minutes to go. He reacted superbly to deny Gary Jones, who had met Junior Mendes' cross from the right with a firm header. Cheltenham had shown great resilience in final weeks of the season and they needed to hold their nerve for the five minutes of time added on, but the whistle finally blew and the promotion party began.

Manager Ward hailed the greatest achievement of his twenty-four-year coaching career after leading Cheltenham Town into the promised land of Coca-Cola League One. The fifty-five-year-old, who had taken charge of Cheltenham in November 2003, had managed Bristol Rovers, Bristol City and York City. He had also been assistant manager at Wolverhampton Wanderers, Burnley, Watford and Aston Villa. He had tasted many highs during his distinguished career, but described this achievement as his greatest. 'I am thrilled with it and it is the best thing I have ever done,' Ward said. 'I am the manager and I have a fantastic group of players who are all working for the same thing. It's taken us two years to get here, which isn't long in football and that's what pleases me most and why I say it's my best achievement.'

Skipper Finnigan described holding the play-off trophy aloft as a 'dream come true.' The Robins captain won at the Millennium Stadium for the second time in four years as Cheltenham overcame Grimsby.

The thirty-year-old was the only remaining member of the Cheltenham team which had triumphed against Rushden in 2002. 'All I could think about was lifting the trophy and it was a great feeling and a dream come true,' he said.

Full-back Gill finally buried his Millennium Stadium demons. The thirty-five-year-old right-back played a starring role in the Grimsby victory. Gill was cruelly dropped by Birmingham City boss Trevor Francis for the final of the 2001 League Cup final after playing in every round in the run to Cardiff.

Cheltenham Town: Higgs, Gill, Caines, Duff, Armstrong (Bell 27), Vincent (Spencer 78), Finnigan, McCann, Wilson, Guinan, Gillespie (Odejayi 62). Subs not used Brown, Bird.
Grimsby Town: Mildenhall, Croft (Futcher 75), R. Jones, Whittle, Newey, Mendes (Goodfellow 83), Woodhouse, Bolland, Parkinson, G. Jones, Reddy (Cohen 27). Subs not used: Kalala, Toner.
Referee: P. Taylor (Herts).
Attendance: 29,196.

MATCH 45: SWANSEA CITY V. CHELTENHAM TOWN

Coca-Cola League One
Saturday 5 August 2006, Liberty Stadium
Swansea City 1 (Knight 77)
Cheltenham Town 2 (Odejayi 48, McCann 54)

Cheltenham Town enjoyed a dream start to their second League One campaign with a stunning win against highly fancied Swansea City on their own patch. Second-half goals from Kayode Odejayi and Grant McCann gave the Robins a 2–0 lead at the Liberty Stadium. Swansea pulled one back through Leon Knight and pushed for an equaliser late on, but John Ward's braves held on for a deserved victory. The Robins – who, with the exception of their centre backs, had the same side that had started last season – showed they would not allow themselves to be bullied against their big-spending and more illustrious opponents in the higher division.

For Cheltenham's first match back in English football's third tier after a three-year absence, Ward handed Jamie Victory his first start since 10 January at left-back, with Craig Armstrong on the left of midfield and Brian Wilson on the bench. Striker Steven Gillespie was fit enough to take his place on the bench, with Odejayi and Steve Guinan paired together up front.

The teams were greeted by a cauldron of noise as they entered the palatial arena, with the vast majority of the 15,000-plus crowd expecting nothing other than a comfortable home win for the Welsh club. However, Cheltenham had developed a habit of defying the odds and after surviving an early onslaught from the previous season's beaten League One play-off finalists that saw Tom Butler force Shane Higgs into a comfortable low save, Cheltenham showed that they were not in the division to make up the numbers. Odejayi appeared to relish his tussle with former Southampton defender Gary Monk and the Nigerian's shot was blocked by Rory Fallon after Guinan had directed a McCann corner back across goal.

Cheltenham did not let the intimidating atmosphere affect them and showed composure and poise on the ball, with JJ Melligan prominent on the right in the opening exchanges. A fine, flowing move involving McCann and Odejayi supplied Melligan and his cross was glanced wide by McCann. For Swansea, Andy Robinson's shot was held by Higgs and the home side's penalty appeals were waved away after Jerry Gill's sliding challenge on Butler in the area. Swansea came within inches of taking the lead after twenty minutes, when Robinson's run took him into the box. After he had stumbled, the ball broke to Butler, whose curling shot appeared to be heading for the bottom right corner with Higgs beaten, but somehow it rebounded off the inside of the post to safety. Butler headed a Robinson cross over the bar and Knight sent a header from Fallon's flick-on wide as Swansea regained the initiative. Higgs parried a well-struck Robinson free-kick after Shane Duff had fouled Knight, and Gill made a sliding block to deny Knight. Duff, who had been feeling unwell in the build-up to the match, was withdrawn at half-time and replaced by Wilson. Victory moved inside to centre-back, with Armstrong reverting to left-back and Wilson operating in his now familiar left-wing role.

Cheltenham stunned Swansea by taking the lead three minutes after the break. John Finnigan dispossessed Butler near the halfway line and floated a perfect diagonal pass to Odejayi, who composed himself and crashed a shot past Willy Gueret and inside the left post. The Swans fans soon began to show their frustration and, although Butler went close with a curling shot, Cheltenham doubled their lead after fifty-four minutes. Guinan helped on a long ball and McCann took advantage of a defensive slip from former Cheltenham loanee Kevin Amankwaah, who cost Swansea more than the entire Robins team put together, and lifted a left-footed effort past the advancing Gueret to

Kayode Odejayi robs Garry Monk.

Grant McCann made it 2–0.

send the travelling fans behind the goal into raptures. Swans boss Kenny Jackett responded quickly by making a triple change, with Kevin McLeod, Leon Britton and Adebayo Akinfenwa replacing Butler, Kristian O'Leary and Fallon. Akinfenwa proved to be a handful with his power, but Victory adjusted to his new position admirably alongside Gavin Caines. Akinfenwa raced on to a long ball, only to see his shot blocked by Higgs. However, Swansea did pull one back after seventy-seven minutes. McLeod reached the goal line and delivered a deep cross from the left which Knight finished at the far post. Odejayi limped off with an ankle injury and was replaced by Ashley Vincent, while Gillespie went on for the tiring Guinan. Wilson burst on to a pass from Vincent inside the area, but his shot was well-blocked by the legs of Gueret, while McCann's audacious thirty-five-yard chip beat Gueret but landed on top of the goal and Vincent shot into the side netting as Cheltenham continued to create chances. Higgs made the save of the match low to his left with five minutes remaining after Akinfenwa had released Knight, and debutant Darren Pratley made a mess of his follow-up attempt. Higgs then held Izzy Iriekpen's header from a Robinson corner on the line, but the Swans could not find another breakthrough and Cheltenham held on for a famous victory.

Swansea City: Gueret, Amankwaah, Iriekpen, Monk, Williams, Robinson, O'Leary (Britton 58), Pratley, Butler (McLeod 58), Knight, Fallon (Akinfenwa 58). Subs not used: Oakes, Austin.
Cheltenham Town: Higgs, Gill, Caines, Duff (Wilson 46), Victory, Melligan, Finnigan, McCann, Armstrong, Guinan (Gillespie 78), Odejayi (Vincent 78). Subs not used: Brown, Bird.
Refereee: S.W. Mathieson (Cheshire).
Attendance: 15,199.

MATCH 46: ROTHERHAM UNITED V. CHELTENHAM TOWN

Coca-Cola League One
Saturday 28 April 2007, Millmoor
Rotherham United 2 (Newsham 14,
  Henderson 22)
Cheltenham Town 4 (Odejayi 44,
  Gillespie 46, 56, Melligan 88)

A club that had achieved so much in the previous decade reached a new high by securing League One safety after an extraordinary comeback at Rotherham United on the penultimate day of the 2006/07 season. Little Cheltenham Town could celebrate in the knowledge they would be welcoming Leeds United to Whaddon Road for a league fixture the following season. When an Eric Cantona-inspired Leeds team won the League Championship at the expense of Manchester United in 1992, the Robins were slipping back into the Southern League from the Conference. A remarkable turnaround in fortunes for both clubs would see them go head to head in League One in 2007/08. Cheltenham had enjoyed four promotions, two victorious play-off final appearances at the Millennium Stadium, an FA Trophy win at Wembley and an FA Cup Fourth Round tie against Newcastle United in the past ten years. However, John Ward's heroes surpassed anything that had gone before them and confirmed their place in Robins folklore by fighting back from two goals down to win in style and guarantee themselves another season in the third tier of English football. Needing three points to be certain of avoiding the drop, the Robins looked set for a nervy clash with Brighton on the final day of the campaign after a nightmare start at Millmoor. Already-relegated Rotherham scored twice in the first half hour, but top scorer Kayode Odejayi's header in the closing seconds of the first half sparked a remarkable recovery at Millmoor.

Rotherham's first was scored by Marc Newsham, who turned sharply and fired a shot into the top right corner after defender Michael Townsend missed a chance to clear his lines after fourteen minutes. The home side's lead was doubled eight minutes later when Delroy Facey's cross from the left was stroked home by Ian Henderson and Cheltenham were in disarray. Millers goalkeeper Gary Montgomery made a fine reaction save from an Odejayi header after Shane Duff had flicked on a long throw from Craig Armstrong. But Odejayi restored hope for Cheltenham when he leapt highest to power JJ Melligan's corner into the net and claim his fifteenth goal in forty-two starts that season. It could have been worse for Cheltenham, but Rotherham had a goal disallowed and stand-in goalkeeper Scott Brown made a crucial save to deny Stephen Brogan during first-half stoppage time and prevent his side falling 3–1 down. With news coming through from Saltergate that Chesterfield were 2–0 up against Bradford City at half time, Cheltenham started the second half knowing that a point would have been enough. They made the best possible start to the second half, shooting towards the travelling Robins fans who were in fine voice all afternoon. Steven Gillespie raced on to a pass from David Bird, poked the ball past the on-rushing Montgomery and ran it into the empty net to level the scores and send Cheltenham on their way to a famous triumph.

A fragile Rotherham defence was then put to the sword by a rampant Robins team, who took the lead for the first time when Gillespie scored his second ten minutes after his first. A long clearance from Brown was brought down by the ever-willing Gavin Caines, who was doing an admirable job in the unfamiliar role of left midfield. The ball fell for Gillespie, who connected perfectly with an unstoppable drive that beat Montgomery and dipped underneath the crossbar. Melligan then produced his party piece to make it 4–2 two minutes from the final whistle. The right midfielder received a pass from Odejayi, flicked the ball up and crashed a fierce drive into the top left corner

Steven Gillespie bagged a brace.

John Ward masterminded the Robins' first survival at League One level.

to register his eighth goal of the campaign. Cheltenham's seventh away success of the season lifted them to seventeenth, which is where they stayed after a final day draw with Brighton, which turned out to be a survival party at Whaddon Road. Ward declared keeping Cheltenham in League One as the finest achievement of his long managerial career. 'When people ask me what this means, the enormity of it is that no team has ever done it before at this football club,' Ward said. 'To do something historic and different as we have done is really special and that's why I say it's the best thing I have ever been involved in.' Ward believed that his constant belief that his team could climb out of the mire had been a key factor. 'When Roger Bannister ran the sub-four minute mile, in the following eighteen months, sixty-eight people did it because they believed it could be done,' he said. 'Now we have done this, I have to get these players to believe they can take the club a little bit further. We have had adversity this season and that is something to overcome, not to accept and we have overcome it.' Gillespie described Cheltenham's win at Rotherham as better than their League Two play-off final success over Grimsby Town eleven months earlier. The twenty-one-year-old striker, who scored twice in the second half, said, 'It tops the Millennium Stadium for me. The play-off final was played in front of nearly 30,000 fans in a massive stadium, but coming to Rotherham with a half-built stadium and getting changed in a portakabin doesn't make any difference. The fans were brilliant and I can't describe how great it feels.'

Rotherham United: Montgomery, Kerr (Wilson 70), Fleming, Sharps, Brogan, Henderson, Jarvis, Cochrane (Keane 61), Woods, Facey, Newsham. Subs not used: O'Grady, Liversidge, Partridge.
Cheltenham Town: Brown, Gill, Townsend, Duff, Armstrong, Melligan, Finnigan, Bird, Caines, Gillespie, Odejayi. Subs not used: Lowe, Connolly, Reid, Yao, Connor.
Referee: S.W. Mathieson (Cheshire).
Attendance: 3,876.

MATCH 47: CHELTENHAM TOWN V. LEEDS UNITED

Coca-Cola League One
Sunday 25 November 2007, Whaddon Road
Cheltenham Town 1 (Gillespie 86)
Leeds United 0

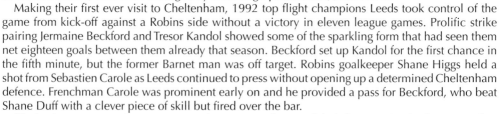

Steven Gillespie's late strike secured one of the finest victories in Cheltenham Town's Football League history against the once-mighty Leeds United. It was a Herculean effort from manager Keith Downing's men against a club steeped in tradition and a team with thirteen wins in their previous sixteen League One outings. The highest crowd assembled at Whaddon Road since April 2002 watched Leeds dominate long periods of the game, but they could not find a way past Cheltenham's well organised backline.

Gillespie capitalised on a misjudgement from Leeds' debutant goalkeeper Dave Lucas in the eighty-sixth minute, guiding a perfectly measured finish into the net from thirty yards to send the home masses into raptures. Not only did the memorable success lift Cheltenham off the foot of the table and up to twenty-first, it also gave Downing his first three-point haul as a senior manager. It was his first triumph in seven games as full-time boss and condemned 2001 European Champions League semi-finalists Leeds to only their second league defeat of the season. Their other reverse was at Carlisle United, who were managed by Downing's predecessor, John Ward.

Making their first ever visit to Cheltenham, 1992 top flight champions Leeds took control of the game from kick-off against a Robins side without a victory in eleven league games. Prolific strike pairing Jermaine Beckford and Tresor Kandol showed some of the sparkling form that had seen them net eighteen goals between them already that season. Beckford set up Kandol for the first chance in the fifth minute, but the former Barnet man was off target. Robins goalkeeper Shane Higgs held a shot from Sebastien Carole as Leeds continued to press without opening up a determined Cheltenham defence. Frenchman Carole was prominent early on and he provided a pass for Beckford, who beat Shane Duff with a clever piece of skill but fired over the bar.

Cheltenham attempted to counter attack at pace and created their first opening in the twenty-first minute when Jerry Gill combined with Paul Connor, whose shot was deflected over for a corner. Only a well-timed intervention from David Bird denied Carole after David Prutton's half-blocked free-kick found its way into the penalty area. Gillespie then found space in the Leeds box after a Bird corner caused problems, but Rui Marques made an important challenge to avert the danger.

Leeds' best attempt of the first half arrived in the thirty-eighth minute when Jonathon Douglas fed ten-goal Beckford, who held off the challenge of Duff, turned sharply and saw his firm drive clip the top of the crossbar. Beckford then missed a golden chance to open the scoring five minutes into the second half when a delicate flick from Kandol played him in on goal. He held off the challenge of the recovering Gavin Caines and lifted the ball over the advancing Higgs, but the ball dropped the wrong side of the near post. Cheltenham responded by carving out a rare opportunity when Ashley Vincent found Gillespie, who cut inside from the right and sent a well-struck effort over Lucas' goal. Another chance fell to Beckford in the sixty-fifth minute when Prutton beat former Leeds loanee Alan Wright in the air at the far post and sent the ball back across goal, but Beckford's first time attempt flew into the stand housing the travelling United fans.

Higgs fell on a Kandol header as Leeds continued to probe, but Beckford could not find his range and sent another shot high over the bar. Leeds boss Dennis Wise sent on Mark De Vries and Tore André Flo in the seventy-third minute in a bid to bolster his side's attacking potency and Beckford had the ball in the net when Higgs spilt a Douglas free-kick in the seventy-sixth minute, but his celebrations were cut short by an offside flag.

Alan Wright was outstanding against his former club.

There was concern for Leeds in the closing minutes when Lucas injured himself in a challenge with Cheltenham's new loan striker Guy Madjo, but he was fit to continue after receiving lengthy treatment. However, Lucas was caught out with four minutes remaining when he rushed off his line to head clear a long ball from Andy Lindegaard. The clearance fell kindly for Gillespie, but he still had a lot to do, dispatching the ball into the net after one bounce and making one of the most unlikely results of the season a reality. The celebrations had barely died down when Gillespie almost added an improbable second, but his cheeky lob drifted wide with Lucas beaten.

Downing was in a jubilant mood after masterminding the most unlikely of victories. The day was doubly special for Downing, who was able to celebrate his first win since taking over as John Ward's full-time successor on 2 November. Steven Gillespie's eighty-sixth-minute goal ended Cheltenham's run of eleven League One games without a victory, lifting them off the foot of the table and up to twenty-first. 'It's been a fantastic day for everyone connected with the club and the town itself,' said Downing, who turned down a chance to join Leeds' coaching staff two years earlier. 'The performance was a resolute one and we rode our luck a little bit, but you are going to have to do that against teams of Leeds' quality. I am pleased for the players because they have kept their belief, their work-rate and their character throughout this difficult period. I don't want this to be a one-off and I am hoping this can kick-start us and that we can have a revival to get back up the league.'

Cheltenham chairman Paul Baker described the win over Leeds United as among the greatest results in the club's history. Baker had overseen the club's progression from non-league part-timers to an established professional outfit competing in English's football's third tier. The Robins had been promoted four times in the previous ten years and had caused many upsets along the way, but Baker said that defeating a club of Leeds' stature matched anything Cheltenham had achieved before. He said, 'This result ranks up there with the great occasions. It's one of those days when you can say "I was there the day Cheltenham Town beat the mighty Leeds United." Leeds' wage bill is probably ten times bigger than ours and in the second half they could bring on Tore André Flo from the bench, who was playing for Chelsea last time I saw him. That puts into perspective what a fantastic result it was.'

Cheltenham Town: Higgs, Gill, Caines, Duff, Wright, Vincent (Lindegaard 72), Bird, Sinclair, Spencer, Connor (Madjo 77), Gillespie. Subs not used: Brown, Gallinagh, D'Agostino.
Leeds United: Lucas, Richardson, Marques, Heath, Parker (De Vries 73), Prutton (Flo 73), Douglas, Hughes, Carole (Westlake 56), Beckford, Kandol. Subs not used: Huntington, Kishishev.
Referee: L.W. Probert (Wiltshire).
Attendance: 7,043 (1,814 from Leeds).

Match 48: Leeds United v. Cheltenham Town

Coca-Cola League One
Tuesday 11 March 2008, Whaddon Road
Leeds United 1 (Elding 85)
Cheltenham Town 2 (Bird 38, Russell 63)

Cheltenham Town chose their most glamorous trip of the 2007/08 season to claim one of the finest results in their history, at Leeds United's Elland Road. With only two away wins all season, Keith Downing's men were convincing 2–1 victors, completing an improbable double over the 2001 European Champions League semi-finalists. The Robins scored once in each half through David Bird and Alex Russell, surviving a late scare to give their chances of avoiding relegation a massive lift at one of the most impressive grounds in English football. Cheltenham made by far the brighter start, forcing three early corners and taking the game to their illustrious hosts. Leeds' best moments were direct counter-attacking sorties after clearing their lines on a boggy Elland Road surface made heavier by a pre-match downpour.

Robins boss Keith Downing made three changes to the side beaten 2–1 at Yeovil Town three days earlier. He also switched formation, opting for a 4-5-1 shape, with leading scorer Steven Gillespie starting on the right wing and Steve Brooker operating alone up front. Damian Spencer was recalled in favour of Andy Lindegaard on the left, while Michael D'Agostino made way to accommodate Alex Russell as the extra central midfielder. At the back, Richard Keogh made his debut alongside Shane Duff in place of Andy Gallinagh. Keogh arrived on loan from Bristol City on Monday to complete a trio of players borrowed from the Coca-Cola Championship leaders. And the central defender was up against two of the most dangerous strikers in League One – seventeen-goal Jermaine Beckford and ten-goal Tresor Kandol. Kandol was presented with the best chance of the first half for Gary McAllister's promotion hopefuls. He reached Bradley Johnson's left wing cross, but contrived to plant a header over the bar when he should have scored, in the twenty-third minute. Leeds may have opened Cheltenham up on that occasion, but the Robins' new formation was proving to be effective, with Gillespie and Spencer causing problems for their opposing full-backs and Brooker a handful in attack. Russell and Spencer both sent shots off target and strong tackles from Duff and Russell showed plenty of passion for the cause. And they were rewarded in the thirty-eighth minute when David Bird robbed a defender after a long kick from Shane Higgs was not dealt with by Leeds. Bird burst forward and calmly placed a low shot into the bottom left corner from twenty yards past goalkeeper Casper Ankergren, who could only stand and watch it roll into the net. Cheltenham attacked again immediately and the previously vociferous home supporters began to voice their discontent as half time approached.

League One's top marksman Beckford received another ball from the left in space, but his shot on the turn flew over the bar. Cheltenham returned to the changing rooms with their noses in front, while Leeds were predictably booed off the field. Higgs did well to beat away a free-kick from Johnson low to his left early in the second half. McAllister sent on recent signing Dougie Freedman in place of Jonny Howson in the sixty-first minute in a bid to find an equaliser. However, Cheltenham stunned the home crowd and doubled their lead two minutes later through a wonderful strike from Russell. Ankergren flapped at Alan Wright's free-kick allowing Duff to pull the ball back to Russell from the goal line. The loan midfielder curled an unstoppable shot into the top right corner from twenty yards to send the travelling Robins fans wild.

Brooker had the ball in the net in the sixty-fifth minute, but the offside flag was up and the striker was presented with a golden chance to score for the fifth time in five games five minutes later. Spencer made a sparkling run down the left and pulled back for Brooker who seemed certain to fire

Damian Spencer had a fine game on the left wing.

Alex Russell is mobbed after his stunning strike at Elland Road.

home into an open goal, but he trod on the ball and will wonder how he failed to score. Russell then struck the woodwork from the edge of the penalty area as a third goal looked a distinct possibility. But Leeds set up a tense finish when Neil Kilkenny's cross was headed in by substitute Anthony Elding from close range with five minutes remaining.

While there was a touch of fortune about Cheltenham's battling 1–0 home win over a dominant Leeds side the previous November, this was a wholly merited success. And it was the sort of performance that suggested there would be League One football at Whaddon Road once again the following season. Keith Downing believed Cheltenham Town's stunning 2–1 win could be their springboard to League One survival as they became the first team to complete a win double over Leeds that season. Downing, who outfoxed Leeds boss Gary McAllister with a tactical masterstroke at Elland Road, described his players as 'heroes' as they defeated the 1992 English League champions on their own turf. 'We should gain immense confidence from this result and the big thing is for this club to stay up and this is a great scalp for us,' Downing said. 'The whole team has contributed and there were a lot of heroes out there tonight. We will enjoy this result, but we have to take this forward now. It's a great win for the town, for the supporters, the directors and the chairman.' Downing made a point of saluting chairman Paul Baker at the final whistle after being allowed to bring in defender Richard Keogh on loan from Bristol City. Keogh made his debut and played his part in a magnificent all-round effort. 'I have to thank the chairman because money is tight at the club, but he has backed me and allowed me to bring another body in,' Downing said. 'I have never lost faith in these boys. I also appreciate the supporters, who have stuck by us through difficult times this season, but they can enjoy nights like these.'

Leeds United: Ankergren, Kenton, Marques, Michalik, Richardson (Hughes 71), Kilkenny, Howson (Freedman 61), Prutton, Johnson, Beckford, Kandol (Elding 71). Subs not used: Lucas, Huntington.
Cheltenham Town: Higgs, Gill, Keogh, Duff, Wright, Gillespie, Bird, Russell, Armstrong, Spencer (Vincent 84), Brooker (Connor 88). Subs not used: S.P. Brown, Lindegaard, D'Agostino.
Referee: C.W. Oliver (Northumberland).
Attendance: 20,257.

MATCH 49: CHELTENHAM TOWN V. DONCASTER ROVERS

Coca-Cola League One
Saturday 3 May 2008, Whaddon Road
Cheltenham Town 2 (Gillespie 24, Connor 85)
Doncaster Rovers 1 (Green 76)

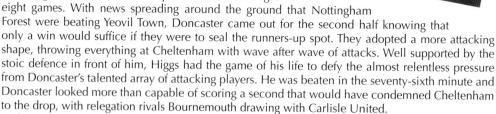

Cheltenham Town preserved their Coca-Cola League One status for the second year in succession on an afternoon of drama to match anything ever witnessed in the long and colourful history of Whaddon Road. The Robins battled to a heroic victory and, in doing so, ended Doncaster Rovers' hopes of automatic promotion. Shane Higgs was the star, producing a breathtaking display of goalkeeping to restrict a dangerous Doncaster side to one goal. The season could not have reached a more gripping climax, but Keith Downing's braves delivered the goods when it really mattered, ending a run of four consecutive defeats to keep themselves away from danger. Fired-up Cheltenham, full of heart and determination, were the better side in the first half and took a twenty-fourth minute lead through in-form goalscorer Steven Gillespie. It was his sixth goal in eight games. With news spreading around the ground that Nottingham Forest were beating Yeovil Town, Doncaster came out for the second half knowing that only a win would suffice if they were to seal the runners-up spot. They adopted a more attacking shape, throwing everything at Cheltenham with wave after wave of attacks. Well supported by the stoic defence in front of him, Higgs had the game of his life to defy the almost relentless pressure from Doncaster's talented array of attacking players. He was beaten in the seventy-sixth minute and Doncaster looked more than capable of scoring a second that would have condemned Cheltenham to the drop, with relegation rivals Bournemouth drawing with Carlisle United.

The complexion of Cheltenham's season was transformed when a rare second-half attack, in the eighty-fifth minute, saw Ashley Vincent pressurise James O'Connor into conceding a corner. Andy Lindegaard's cross caused mayhem in the Rovers penalty area, with Richard Keogh winning a header before O'Connor cleared, but only as far as Shane Duff. Duff set himself and carefully fired the ball towards the line, where Connor slid in to stab home a goal that lifted the roof off Whaddon Road. The atmosphere before kick-off was as electric as it was tense, with both sides' seasons boiling

down to ninety minutes of drama. Downing initiated a new pre-match huddle involving all of his players and backroom staff and the home fans responded with an expectant roar. A high-octane forty-five minutes followed for Cheltenham as they carved out several early chances without testing Doncaster's Scottish international 'keeper Neil Sullivan. There were some clear signs of nerves from both teams, with some simple passes going astray and players running the ball out of play under no pressure from the opposition.

Paul Connor's late strike eased the intense pressure at Whaddon Road.

Cheltenham Town get the party started after overcoming the odds to avoid relegation for the second year in succession.

A Gillespie shot on the turn was held by Sullivan, diving to his right, but Cheltenham took a deserved lead midway through the half. Gillespie's goals kept Cheltenham alive during the second half of the campaign and once again he demonstrated the ability to create something from a half chance. Alex Russell chipped a pass in behind the Doncaster back four and Connor found Gillespie, who beat Sullivan with a clever finish from eight yards out. Keogh volleyed wide after a Russell corner, but Higgs was tested for the first time in the thirty-fifth minute when he denied Sam Hird before Gillespie hacked Gareth Taylor's effort off the line to ensure the Robins led at half-time.

The second half was all Doncaster, with Higgs denying Roberts in the forty-ninth minute and then stopping a firm header from Taylor. Alan Wright made a vital challenge to rob substitute Jason Price as he shaped to shoot, but the Robins' goal was under siege and was finally breached. Brian Stock's cross was headed down by Price and Paul Green crashed the ball home. Roberts' cross was helped on by Green to Paul Heffernan, who was denied by the legs of Higgs and Price rolled a shot against the far post with Higgs a spectator, as the tension became almost unbearable. It seemed only a matter of time before Rovers struck again, but Cheltenham hit them with a sucker punch five minutes from the end. Connor's fifth goal of the season ensured that the Robins did not have to rely on other results to guarantee safety. The striker relieved the intense pressure that had been building up around Whaddon Road. It rendered relegation rivals Gillingham's result at Leeds United and Bournemouth's at Carlisle United irrelevant. Higgs then made an outstanding save to push Heffernan's header from Roberts' cross around a post. Green drew yet another tremendous stop from Higgs deep into stoppage time as an emotionally exhausting contest drew to a close. Cheltenham celebrated with a mixture of elation and relief.

Downing had taken over from John Ward early in the season and poured his heart and soul into achieving what looked like an impossible task at Christmas. He admitted he felt totally drained after finally completing the club's objective for the season. 'I have absolutely nothing left and it's been a real emotional rollercoaster, but a great day,' he said. 'We have put our bodies on the line and it's just what we are as a club because it was all Doncaster in the second half, but it typifies this group of players that we held out for the win. People have written us off, but we keep defying the odds and there is a special group of people working here. This is a better achievement than staying up last year because of what this club has been through.'

Cheltenham Town: Higgs, Gill, Duff, Keogh, Wright, S. Brown (Lindegaard 60), Bird, Russell (Armstrong 73), Vincent, Connor, Gillespie. Subs not used: S.P. Brown, Connolly, Armstrong, D'Agostino.
Doncaster Rovers: Sullivan, O'Connor, Hird, Mills, Roberts, Green, Stock, Wellens, Coppinger (Guy 75), Taylor (Price 61), McCammon (Heffernan 75). Subs not used: Lee, Hayter, Price.
Referee: L.S. Mason (Lancashire).
Attendance: 6,787.

MATCH 50: CHELTENHAM TOWN V. PETERBOROUGH UNITED

Coca-Cola League One
Sunday 28 December 2008, Whaddon Road
Cheltenham Town 3 (Vincent 48 pen,
  Hammond 67, Owusu 86)
Peterborough United 6 (Boyd 3, Lee 60,
  Mackail-Smith 63, Wright 75og, Mclean 87,
  Whelpdale 90)

A depleted Cheltenham Town side finished what was a highly eventful calendar year of 2008 with an astonishing 6–3 defeat at the hands of eventual League One runners-up Peterborough United in an enthralling contest. Shorn of a host of first-team regulars, the Robins could not live with a classy Peterborough side and their unbeaten run of six games was brought to an abrupt end at Whaddon Road. Peterborough took an early lead, but it remained 1–0 until half time. Seven goals followed in the final half an hour as the Robins battled bravely, but Darren Ferguson's Posh had too much quality up front for Cheltenham's makeshift defence to cope with. It was the first time Cheltenham had shipped six goals or more since the 7–0 Carling Cup second round defeat at Crystal Palace in 2002.

The visitors almost scored in the first minute when Alex Russell carelessly gave the ball away inside his own half and George Boyd forced Scott Brown into a smart save. Boyd made no mistake in the third minute, however, firing in Craig Mackail-Smith's square ball via a heavy deflection off Andy Gallinagh's foot that lifted the ball over the helpless Brown.

Cheltenham were missing six players through injury and illness and transfer-listed Josh Low was handed his first league start since 20 September, against his former club. Despite the under-strength side, the Robins recovered from their early setback and matched their in-form opponents for the rest of the first half. Posh goalkeeper Joe Lewis came to claim a long throw from Lee Ridley, but he failed to gather the ball cleanly, presenting Ashley Vincent with a free shot on goal. However, Craig Morgan hacked off the line. Peterborough, who started the day in sixth place and had lost just one of their previous sixteen games, had the ball in the net again in the twelfth minute when Mackail-Smith turned in Boyd's pass, only for his effort to be ruled out for offside.

Vincent made a lively start for Cheltenham and he received an incisive pass from Russell, but could not trouble Lewis with his shot. Russell lost possession again in the thirty-first minute and the dangerous Boyd set up Mackail-Smith, who had only Brown to beat, but the Robins goalkeeper made another fine block. Westlake released Ridley on the left with a measured pass and the left-back's cross was met by Elvis Hammond, but Lewis was able to catch comfortably under the bar. Brown held a shot from Boyd after Alan Wright's timely clearance in the forty-first minute. Wright, 5ft 4in, was playing in the centre of defence after his spell in the centre of midfield at Yeovil Town on Boxing Day.

After doing well to stay with their opponents before half time, Cheltenham levelled three minutes into the second half. Hammond combined with Westlake to set up Vincent, who was bundled over by Charlie Lee inside the penalty area and a spot-kick was awarded. Vincent stepped up to send Lewis the wrong way, netting his fifth goal of the season and his fourth in five games to take over as the Robins' leading scorer in his own right. Brown made another one-on-one save to keep out Aaron McClean after an hour and from the resulting corner, Lee made up for his indiscretion for the penalty by powering in a header from Dean Keates' corner over Wright on the line. Vincent felt he was impeded by Lee as he jumped for the ball and was shown a yellow card for dissent. Peterborough added their third goal three minutes later when Mackail-Smith burst through on to McClean's

*Elvis Hammond
watches his first goal
for Cheltenham hit
the back of the net.*

header, rounded the advancing Brown and finished calmly past Wright on the line. Hammond scored his first goal for the Robins to reduce the deficit and restore hope in the sixty-seventh minute. Gallinagh robbed Boyd and fed Vincent on the right wing, who sent the ball in early low towards Hammond. He beat his man and fired in a low finish.

Peterborough ended the game as a contest in the seventy-fifth minute when Mackail-Smith got the better of Kenton and Vincent on the left and the unfortunate Wright put the ball into his own net from close range. Boyd had a glorious chance to make it 5–2 in the eighty-first minute, but Brown made another miraculous save. Substitute Lloyd Owusu then scored his fifth goal of the season in the eighty-sixth minute after a long throw from Ridley caused havoc, but McClean went straight up the other end to make it 5–3 from the restart.

Hayles had endured a frustrating afternoon and was sent off for stamping on Tom Williams in the third minute of time added on, and the striker would then miss four matches, including the FA Cup third-round tie against Doncaster Rovers on the following Saturday.

Peterborough looked capable of scoring with every attack and Chris Whelpdale forced in number six at the far post in the ninety-fifth minute. Manager Martin Allen defended his players after watching them succumb to a rampant Peterborough side. 'A lot of credit has to go to our players and I don't think 6–3 was a fair reflection,' he said. 'They have two outstanding centre-forwards [Craig Mackail-Smith and Aaron McClean] and we pushed forward for more goals and got caught on the counter-attack. I have no complaints about my players and I thought they were absolutely fantastic.'

Cheltenham Town: Brown, Gallinagh (Owusu 72), Wright, Kenton, Ridley, Low, Russell, Westlake, Hammond (Hayes 90) Hayles, Vincent. Subs not used: Connor, Lindegaard, Puddy.
Peterborough United: Lewis, Martin, Morgan, Lee, Williams, Whelpdale, Coutts (Crofts 86), Keates, Boyd, Mackail-Smith, McClean. Subs not used: Westwood, Batt, Green, Blanchett.
Referee: P. Miller (Bedfordshire).
Attendance: 3,976 (504 from Peterborough).

50 Classic Matches

Saturday 9 December 1933, Brunton Park	Carlisle United 1 (Slinger) Cheltenham Town 2 (Smith, Bradley og)	FA Cup Second Round
Saturday 13 January 1934, Cheltenham Athletic Ground	Cheltenham Town 1 (Payne 5) Blackpool 3 (Bussey, Watson 59 pen, Doherty 77)	FA Cup Third Round
Saturday 17 November 1956, Whaddon Road	Cheltenham Town 1 (McAllister 15) Reading 2 (Dixon 44, 77)	FA Cup First Round
Saturday 19 April 1958, Whaddon Road	Cheltenham Town 2 (Cleland 23, Fowler 33) Gravesend & Northfleet 1 (Thomas 75)	Southern League Cup Final, second leg
Monday 22 January 1979, Moss Lane	Altrincham 1 (Rogers 60) Cheltenham Town 2 (Brown 1, 10)	FA Trophy First Round
Saturday 2 October 1982, Whaddon Road	Cheltenham Town 5 (Abbley 9, Dyer 30, Lewis 34, 75, Gough 82) Gloucester City 1 (Williams)	FA Cup second qualifying round
Saturday 4 May 1985, Whaddon Road	Cheltenham Town 2 (Boyland, Hughes pen) Alvechurch 1	Southern League Premier Division
Saturday 14 November1987, Molineux	Wolves 5 (Vaughan 23, Bull 27, 62, 83, Downing 46) Cheltenham 1 (Angell 20)	FA Cup First Round
Saturday 17 November 1990, St Andrews	Birmingham City 1 (Sturridge 57) Cheltenham Town 0	FA Cup First Round
Saturday 14 November 1992, Clarence Park	St Albans 1 (Duffield 56 pen) Cheltenham Town 2 (Willetts 61 pen, Purdie 72)	FA Cup First Round
Saturday 5 December 1992, Whaddon Road	Cheltenham Town 1 (Warren 83) AFC Bournemouth 1 (Shearer 12)	FA Cup Second Round
Monday 12 April 1993, Meadow Park	Gloucester City 1 (Penny 87) Cheltenham Town 5 (Howells 7, Bloomer 40, Eaton 62, J. Smith 83 pen, Howells 87)	Beazer Homes League Premier Division
Saturday 27 August 1994, Whaddon Road	Cheltenham Town 8 (Howells 12, Boyle 18, 51, 54, Smith 23, 40, 78, Eaton, 72) Corby Town 0	Beazer Homes League Premier Division
Saturday 29 October 1994, Whaddon Road	Cheltenham Town 6 (Eaton 16, 59, 74, Cooper 34, Boyle 56) Hastings Town 0	Beazer Homes League Premier Division
Saturday 26 December 1994, Meadow Park	Gloucester City 1 (Crowley 73) Cheltenham Town 2 (Warren 46, Eaton 52)	Beazer Homes League Premier Division
Saturday 11 March 1995, Whaddon Road	Cheltenham Town 2 (Boyle 6, Smith 52) Hednesford Town 0	Beazer Homes League Premier Division
Monday 8 April 1996, Meadow Park	Gloucester City 0 Cheltenham Town 3 (Eaton 56, 74, Elsey 73)	Dr Marten's League Premier Division
Tuesday 29 October 1996, Whaddon Road	Cheltenham Town 4 (Boyle 90, Eaton 91, Smith 93, Howells 110) Bath City 1 (Davis 35)	FA Cup fourth qualifying round replay
Saturday 16 November 1996 London Road	Peterborough United 0 Cheltenham Town 0	FA Cup First Round
Saturday 29 March 1997, The Grove	Halesowen Town 1 (Freeman og 31) Cheltenham Town 5 (Knight 60, Dunwell 73, 75 pen, Wright 81, Boyle 87)	Dr Marten's League Premier Division
Saturday 3 May 1997, Eton Park	Burton Albion 0 Cheltenham Town 0	Dr Marten's League Premier Division
Saturday 1 November 1998, Whaddon Road	Cheltenham Town 4 (Eaton 61, 62, 72, Bloomer 67) Halifax Town 0	GM Vauxhall Conference
Tuesday 13 January 1998, Whaddon Road	Cheltenham Town 1 (Watkins 23 pen) Reading 1 (Morley 71)	FA Cup Third Round
Saturday 4 April 1998, The Crabble Athletic Ground	Dover Athletic 2 (Le Bihan 70, Budden 78) Cheltenham Town 2 (Watkins 6, Eaton 33)	FA Trophy Semi-Final, second leg
Sunday 17 May 1998, Wembley Stadium	Cheltenham Town 1 (Eaton 79) Southport 0	FA Umbro Trophy Final
Saturday 3 April 1999, Nene Park	Rushden & Diamonds 1 (de Souza 21) Cheltenham Town 2 (Freeman 90, Grayson 90)	Nationwide Conference

Thursday 22 April 1999, Whaddon Road	Cheltenham Town 3 (Victory 4, Grayson 22, Duff 90) Yeovil Town 2 (Pickard 2, Patmore 47 pen)	Nationwide Conference
Saturday 7 August 1999, Field Mill	Mansfield Town 0 Cheltenham Town 1 (Grayson 64)	Nationwide League Division Three
Tuesday 24 August 1999, Whaddon Road	Cheltenham Town 2 (Grayson 47 pen, Victory 70) Norwich City 1 (L. Marshall 100)	Worthington Cup first round, second leg
Saturday 2 December 2000, Whaddon Road	Cheltenham Town 4 (McAuley 9, 36, Alsop 62, 89) Barnet 3 (Currie 25, Cottee 27, Riza 60)	Nationwide League Division Three
Saturday 17 February 2001, Whaddon Road	Cheltenham Town 3 (McCann 8, Alsop 11, Bloomer 70) Brighton & HA 1 (Cullip 14)	Nationwide League Division Three
1 April 2001, Whaddon Road	Cheltenham Town 3 (Grayson 37, 41, 49) Cardiff City 1 (Young 6)	Nationwide League Division Three
Saturday 6 January 2002, Whaddon Road	Cheltenham Town 2 (Naylor 25, 60) Oldham Athletic 1 (Eyres 43)	FA Cup Third Round
Sunday 27 January 2002, Whaddon Road	Cheltenham Town 2 (Milton 23, Alsop 27) Burnley 1 (A. Moore 29)	FA Cup Fourth Round
Saturday 16 February 2002, The Hawthorns	West Bromwich Albion 1 (Dichio 64) Cheltenham Town 0	FA Cup Fifth Round
Tuesday 30 April 2002, Whaddon Road	Cheltenham Town 1 (Williams 26) Hartlepool United 1 (Arnison 17) (Cheltenham won 5–4 on pens)	Nationwide League Division Three play-off semi-final, second leg
Monday 6 May 2002, Millennium Stadium	Cheltenham Town 3 (Devaney 27, Alsop 49, Finnigan 80) Rushden & Diamonds 1 (Hall 28)	Nationwide League DivisionThree play-off final
Tuesday 10 September 2002, Carrow Road	Norwich City 0 Cheltenham Town 3 (Naylor 30,45, McAuley 83)	Worthington Cup first round
Friday 5 September 2003, Whaddon Road	Cheltenham Town 4 (Taylor 56, Forsyth 76 pen, 90 pen, Devaney 90) Northampton Town 3 (Dudfield 24, 32, Smith 73 pen)	Nationwide League Division Three
Saturday 6 March 2004, Whaddon Road	Cheltenham Town 3 (McCann 32, Finnigan 87, Odejayi 90) Lincoln City 2 (Richardson 3, 45 pen)	Nationwide League Division Three
Saturday 28 January 2006, Whaddon Road	Cheltenham Town 0 Newcastle United 2 (Chopra 41, Parker 43)	FA Cup Fourth Round
Saturday 6 May 2006, Field Mill	Mansfield Town 0 Cheltenham Town 5 (Gillespie 34, Vincent 45, McCann 50, Bird 81pen, Odejayi 85)	Coca-Cola League Two
Saturday 13 May 2006, Adams Park	Wycombe Wanderers 1 (Mooney 90) Cheltenham Town 2 (Finnigan 43, Guinan 75)	Coca-Cola League Two play-off semi-final, first leg
Sunday 28 May 2006, Millennium Stadium	Cheltenham Town 1 (Guinan 63) Grimsby Town 0	Coca-Cola League Two play-off final
Saturday 5 August 2006, Liberty Stadium	Swansea City 1 (Knight 77) Cheltenham Town 2 (Odejayi 48, McCann 54)	Coca-Cola League One
Saturday 28 April 2007, Millmoor	Rotherham United 2 (Newsham 14, Henderson 22) Cheltenham Town 4 (Odejayi 44, Gillespie 46, 56, Melligan 88)	Coca-Cola League One
Sunday 25 November 2007, Whaddon Road	Cheltenham Town 1 (Gillespie 86) Leeds United 0	Coca-Cola League One
Tuesday 11 March 2008, Whaddon Road	Leeds United 1 (Elding 85) Cheltenham Town 2 (Bird 38, Russell 63)	Coca-Cola League One
Saturday 3 May 2008, Whaddon Road	Cheltenham Town 2 (Gillespie 24, Connor 85) Doncaster Rovers 1 (Green 76)	Coca-Cola League One
Sunday 28 December 2008, Whaddon Road	Cheltenham Town 3 (Vincent 48 pen, Hammond 67, Owusu 86) Peterborough United 6 (Boyd 3, Lee 60, Mackail-Smith 63, Wright 75og, Mclean 87, Whelpdale 90)	Coca-Cola League One

Also available from The History Press

Cheltenham Town FC: 50 Greats
Jon Palmer and Tom Goold
978-07524-4150-4

Cheltenham Town FC Since 1970
Peter Matthews
978-07524-3154-3

www.thehistorypress.co.uk